CW00429652

CATALYSE

Praise for the Book

The book is a refreshingly straightforward and practical read that focuses on jobs to be done and business outcomes, rather than on complex process. It brings together practical insights from several organizations and is a good read for business and HR professionals alike.

—**Wayne Hoare**
Chief Human Resources Officer, InterContinental Hotels Group

Aligning human capital with strategic business acumen will be the defining capabilities of business leaders going forward. Businesses need to inspire people whilst continuing to drive growth. *Catalyse* sets out how you can ensure that human potential runs throughout your business, guaranteeing that people are at the heart of leadership. This book will be a great tool for business leaders to understand how to leverage their people power.

—**Leena Nair**
Chief Human Resources Officer, Unilever

Krish Shankar's book could not have come at a better time, when major disruptions stare at businesses and the world of work. His practical and interactive narrative on positive psychology, leadership behaviours and work culture delivers on its promise—lending insightful ideas on maximizing human potential, something that lies at the core of strong businesses and successful leaders. The book maintains the right balance of winning experiences from the past and maxims for creating a sustainable yet strong future while bringing the three most important ingredients of HR together—talent, culture and inclusivity. It provides the right recipe required to reimagine the workplace for tomorrow—one that is steady yet agile, efficient yet resilient, and balances both human and digital.

—**Sanjiv Mehta**
Chairman and Managing Director, Hindustan Unilever Ltd,
President, Unilever South Asia

Shankar's approach to discussing ideas, concepts and practices of HR is refreshing and relevant. The new capability framework 'SBEM' [skills, behaviours, experiences and mindset] is a huge leap in thinking that could significantly alter our approach to talent. The book is not just a reflection of the author's rich experience and erudition but a true reflection of his personality—authentic, elegant and caring. It is an ace!

—**Dr Santrupt Misra**
Group Director, Carbon Black;
Director, Chemicals and Director, Group Human Resources,
Aditya Birla Group

As HR practitioners, two of the most common questions that we get asked are: 'What is the business impact being created through HR processes?' and 'How are we creating value?' We have also seen several well-intentioned HR initiatives and processes failing, as employees do not adopt them. Krish Shankar's book *Catalyse—Power Up Your People Ecosystem* helps address these questions in a simple and practical way. Drawn from experiences and with real world insights, this book is a must-read for professionals who want to make a difference in business.

With rapid shifts in the way work is done, workplaces are being re-envisioned and with shifting workforce demographics, it is absolutely necessary for HR professionals to stay ahead of the curve. Theoretical models and processes that run in silos no longer have any place in organizations. The book aptly calls out the need to move beyond functional silos to an outcome-based framework. It will equip HR professionals to don the organization hat and look beyond the function to create solutions for business problems.

I have personally implemented the 'jobs to be done' framework and seen its impact on business growth. As explained in this book, applying this concept to people and organizational work will help move the function from value enabler to value creator.

—**Archana Bhaskar**
Chief Human Resources Officer, Dr Reddy's Laboratories Ltd

CATALYSE

POWER UP YOUR PEOPLE ECOSYSTEM

KRISH SHANKAR

Best wishes

RUPA

Published by
Rupa Publications India Pvt. Ltd 2021
7/16, Ansari Road, Daryaganj
New Delhi 110002

Sales Centres:
Allahabad Bengaluru Chennai
Hyderabad Jaipur Kathmandu
Kolkata Mumbai

Illustrations: Tanmay Vora

ISBN: 978-93-5520-116-4

Second impression 2022

10 9 8 7 6 5 4 3 2

Printed at Sanat Printers, India

Contents

Foreword

I am not a superstitious person, but I do believe in coincidences.

The request to write a foreword for Krish Shankar's excellent book on human relations (HR) came to me at a time when I was, coincidentally, seeking an answer to a the question: how can chief executive officers (CEOs) develop a more proactive approach to a company's orientation to people?

This question arose in my mind following a research project. I had an engagement with five academics of Bharatiya Vidya Bhavan's S.P. Jain Institute of Management and Research (SPJIMR), Mumbai, on an ongoing three-year applied research project. The project was seeking an answer to the following question: what distinctive MBAs—mindset, behaviour, action—do institutional business builders deploy in contrast to good CEOs of good companies?

We studied Deepak Parekh's role at HDFC, Uday Kotak's at Kotak Mahindra Bank, Harsh Mariwala's at Marico, S. Ramadorai's at TCS, Kiran Mazumdar-Shaw's at Biocon and A.M. Naik's at L&T. My co-researchers and I wrote a book each on these six institutions. Our research found that institutional shapers practise eight 'MBAs', the primary one being the People Mindset-Behaviour-Action. The books, of course, described how these shapers practised the People MBA, along with the other seven MBAs.

This foreword is not about my research project, so let me cut to the chase. Every time I spoke about the research findings and the books, somebody in the audience would ask, 'The People MBA speaks for itself, it is a self-evident truth, but how should a leadership team execute the People MBA? Can you recommend a book on that?' That was the question I was wrestling with.

And then came Krish Shankar's manuscript, almost as an answer to the question!

This book should be read by any corporate leader who wishes to transform a good company into a potentially great business institution. The leadership team should brief the chief human resource officer (CHRO) to execute the People MBA as per the workbook approach contained in Shankar's book. While HR books are often written as though the subject is a functional silo, I suggest this one because the content is designed to bring a results-and-outcome focus to HR.

The book is practical and workmanlike. It also explores contemporary concepts of positive psychology in the subject of HR itself—new ideas on emotions, happiness and growth mindset. It also suggests a new framework for HR professionals based on three distinct roles: designer of an inclusive organization, architect of emotions and culture and a partner with regard to talent. In addition, operating leaders have shared their own perspectives through the chapters to make the content relevant to line managers. Which is why this is a book for budding business managers and for every HR person.

It will be a long journey of seeking the Holy Grail, but, for sure, it will be rewarding. This book may not read like a novel, nor was it intended to. It contains the *brahma-mantra* of how to practise People Mindset-Behaviour-Action in the journey of transforming a good company into an institution.

20 February 2021
Mumbai

R. Gopalakrishnan
Author and Corporate Advisor

Introduction
Blowin' in the Wind

'One more book on business? I have seen so many of these. What's this really about? Is it of any use?' These are the thoughts that come to my mind when I see any new book on the subject. So, let me try to articulate what this book is about, and you can gauge if it caters to your interest.

Many of you are heading businesses and organizations. And, many of you might be aspiring to do so. As you grow in your career and take on bigger responsibilities, you realize that a big part of your success lies in getting the best out of your people. The people element can be split into two: what you can get done through your personal leadership style, and how you can leverage people systems and processes to maximize the human potential.

The following diagram captures the key elements needed for the success of any business leader.

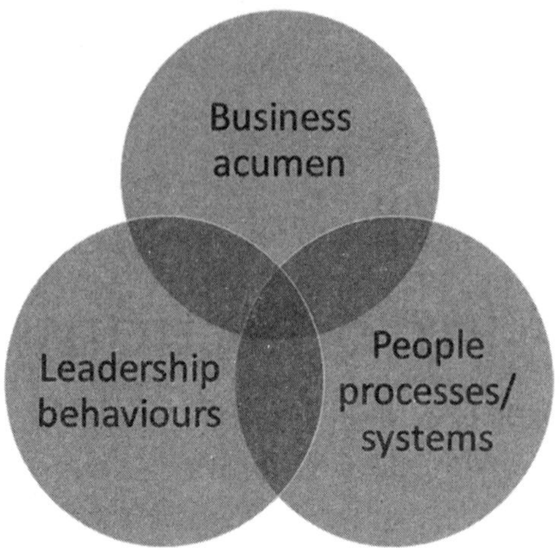

The first ingredient that will drive your success as a business leader is your strategic acumen, and an understanding of the business and insights into its levers. The second is your leadership style—inspiring people, getting the team together and driving results. There is no dearth of literature in these two areas, and you have probably read quite a few books on the subject. However, the more responsible you are for all aspects of a business or the higher you go up the traditional hierarchy, the greater comes into play a key third element that enables business success, an element for which most people don't prepare. It is about how you leverage your people processes, systems and routines to maximize the human potential in your organization. Your personal leadership style can impact only a small number of people directly, and may not change the entire organization. You can create a larger impact only if you can architect your human process ecosystem appropriately and make sure that every person in the organization demonstrates the right behaviours and actions for the success of the business. That will be the focus of this book—how we can build the right people-related outcomes through processes and systems that will enable the business to success. It is what we call HR.

Apart from the above three elements of success, there is another elusive one—luck. Frankly, it remains underestimated. But if we are prepared for the first three elements, luck should follow.

Let us take the case of John, a newly minted CEO of a consumer goods company. He had a wonderful track record of success as a sales and marketing leader, but took over as a CEO when the company had a flattish revenue growth. He firmly believed that a modification of the incentive bonus scheme would change the course of the company for the better. And so he went about implementing an aggressive bonus plan. The first year was positive as sales grew. In the second year, he spotted some warning signs. His top team was not very collaborative, and there was a lot of jostling involved before he could get everyone to agree to the goals and targets for the year. Sales slowed down and the trade was overstocked. John was under major performance pressure.

What had happened? It had been a classic case of myopic thinking. Without understanding all the elements of the goal-setting process and the long-term impact of an aggressive bonus plan on the behaviour of managers, John was blindly wedded to his idea and forced it through. A better understanding of the nuances of the goal-setting, performance management and reward processes would have avoided the damage.

I am reminded of my own experience when I first went to Unilever in 1997 to join the corporate HR team. My first project was to lead a cross-continent team to build a development resources framework and guide for the Unilever competencies. The first two meetings ended in several disparate discussions and we got nowhere. I was struggling to get the team aligned and didn't have much clarity on what we ought to be doing and how one might achieve that in a global organization. I was headed for a disaster. My boss got one of the consultants we worked with to coach me. I started to understand the science better and, more importantly, learnt how to introduce a framework that works across many countries. We finally ended up doing a decent job. Nonetheless, when I reflect on it, I wish I had been better prepared, with a better understanding of issues across cultures.

Therefore, to get the best out of your people, you need two key things—the appropriate leadership behaviours and a deep understanding of people systems, with ideas on leveraging them to maximize human potential. And this book is about the latter. But why has it become more important now? We never gave such weightage to it in the past and normally picked it up on the job.

Two key reasons for why it is so critical now to understand ways to maximize human potential through people systems and outcomes present themselves. The first is that, in the past, many of the leaders grew for a long time in a particular company before they became business heads. This allowed them to learn about the HR systems in their respective organizations and also figure out ways to get around them. But things are changing now. More people are moving jobs far more frequently and are taking on end-to-end business roles earlier on in their careers than before. We now have more start-ups where leaders may not have had enough exposure to people systems. Business contexts are also changing, and we have shorter runways to show results.

The second reason is that the whole area of HR has seen a lot of change over the last decade. It is also probably one field of expertise that will undergo further change in the next couple of decades, given the shifts in people's attitudes, society and in technology. The pandemic has reinforced this belief. What HR will do in the future will be very different from its present activities. We have always looked at HR from a purely functional perspective—recruitment, training, performance management, etc. But the world of work is changing. HR is becoming more integrated in everything we do. And it pays to be ahead of the curve in terms of our understanding of how we look at things and what would work.

Much like the significance of corporate culture, the importance of people and people-related outcomes in the success of a business will continue to rise, since the only true differentiator of a business will be its culture and people. The COVID pandemic of 2020 has also been an inflection point. Every company is revisiting assumptions about work—about how we work and about the workforce. Moreover, if you analyse the composition of the drivers of GDP growth over the last few decades and estimate for the future, it is clear that the quality of talent, not the quantity (of both talent and capital), will be the biggest growth driver. Therefore, the role of HR shall be paramount in value creation.

This book offers a distinct perspective on traditional HR. For one, it focuses on linking people-related outcomes to your business objectives in a simple and clear manner. Importantly, it focuses on outcomes, or what one would like done, rather than on functional processes. And finally, it looks at people outcomes in the context of the future—in a world that would be marked by an ever-enhancing technology, where workplaces are going to be very different from that of the past and where the adaptation of new insights from behavioural research becomes increasingly relevant.

Value in organizations is created by a series of initiatives and actions linked to the strategy of the organization, a series of 'jobs to be done' to realize value. Borrowing the concept of the jobs to be done, which was articulated by Prof Clayton M. Christensen, the famous Harvard professor known for his theory on innovations and how companies fail (author of *The Innovator's Dilemma*) we will look at HR from that perspective. In his book, *Competing Against Luck*, Prof. Christensen talks about the case of a fast food business which developed a smoothie that the firm thought would be ideal for kids who return from school and snack in the evening. However, it found that the smoothie was selling more during the day. On further study, the firm's executives noticed that the smoothie was actually being bought by people driving to office; they wanted something filling that they could snack on while they drove and the smoothie fitted that role admirably.[1]

Therefore, we need to understand what jobs people want to get done at different points in time, and then design products to meet those needs. Similarly, when organizations set out on their quest to create value, it would be good to look at what jobs need to get done to realize that value. That's the cornerstone of how this book is structured. It would look at people and people-related outcomes through a new lens—different from the traditional HR—with a view to maximize the potential of people. It shuns the traditional silos that dog the function and looks at end-to-end actions to deliver the appropriate people outcomes. Well, I guess you have to read on further to discover what the difference is!

Let me now try to summarize these introductory thoughts in a couple of formulas.

What are the determinants of success for a business leader?

Successful business leader/CEO = her strategic business acumen x getting the best out of people

How does one get the best out of people?

Maximize people potential = her demonstrated leadership behaviour x her ability to get right people-related outcomes

Why is it important for a business to get the right people-related outcomes?

Importance of getting the right people outcomes = f (rate of change in the business + changes in people's and societal attitudes) x increasing importance of people in a business's success

As the above equation states, given the fast-paced changes in the business and in people's attitudes, the importance of securing the right people outcomes becomes ever more important.

Finally, this book tries to offer a new perspective to traditional HR processes. We will look at them from the perspective of 'people outcomes' needed to achieve certain business objectives, introduce new insights from research and bring practical knowledge from various industry leaders who were interviewed during the course of writing the book. The answer is blowing in the wind!

To the budding HR professional, this could provide a fresh outlook and help connect the dots. It could also give one a new lexicon to engage with the business, if one were looking to increase one's effectiveness in that area. We are all in this learning journey, and can hopefully keep adding as we go along.

I would like to emphasise that this book is not about preaching—everyone has their own insights and experiences that they can build on. I don't think I can claim to be an HR guru; there are many who are better and more accomplished than me. I am writing this more to share my learning and reflections, build a common understanding and a body of knowledge for the larger community. This book is about sharing my perspectives so you don't have to make the same mistakes that I did. This is my way of expressing gratitude for all that people have taught me.

Look at this book as a mentor. It could facilitate coaching and nudge you to look at things differently. It can also help build your ability to leverage your people potential.

It's time to prepare for the age of human potential maximization. More success to you!

Reference

1. Clayton M. Christensen, *Competing Against Luck: The Story of Innovation and Customer Choice,* Harper Business, 2016.

1

Take It to the Limit

Understanding New Contexts

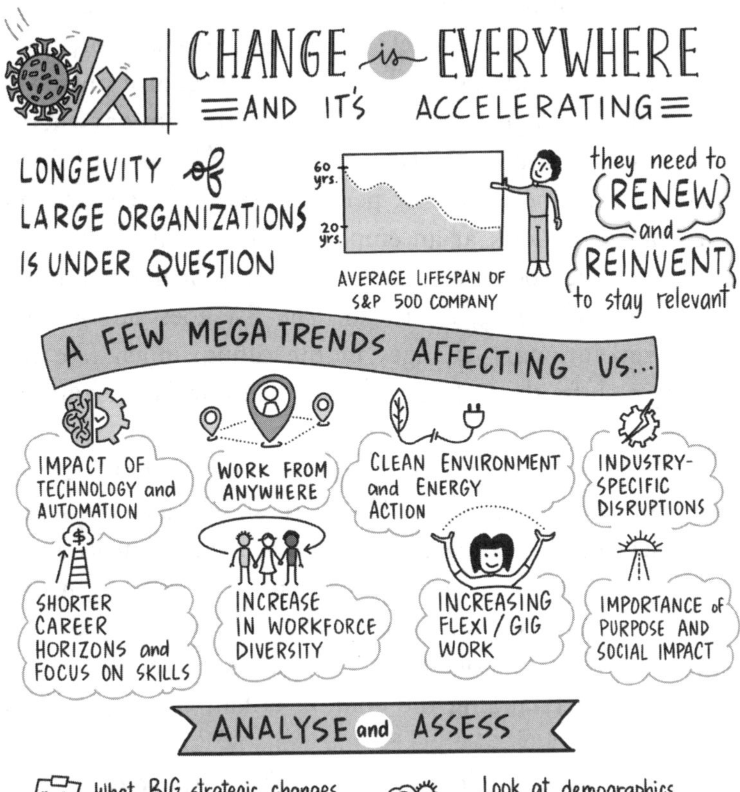

CHANGE is EVERYWHERE
AND IT'S ACCELERATING
LONGEVITY of LARGE ORGANIZATIONS IS UNDER QUESTION
60 yrs.
20 yrs.
AVERAGE LIFESPAN OF S&P 500 COMPANY
they need to RENEW and REINVENT to stay relevant
A FEW MEGA TRENDS AFFECTING US...
IMPACT OF TECHNOLOGY and AUTOMATION
WORK FROM ANYWHERE
CLEAN ENVIRONMENT and ENERGY ACTION
INDUSTRY-SPECIFIC DISRUPTIONS
$
SHORTER CAREER HORIZONS and FOCUS ON SKILLS
INCREASE IN WORKFORCE DIVERSITY
INCREASING FLEXI / GIG WORK
IMPORTANCE of PURPOSE AND SOCIAL IMPACT
ANALYSE and ASSESS
What BIG strategic changes can happen in our industry and in our adjacent industries?
Look at demographics and skills of workforce
Identify 'archetypal' personas that are present

WHAT CHANGES DO YOU EXPECT IN YOUR WORKFORCE?

We survived 2020 and the COVID pandemic, but it did unhinge some of our assumptions about work and the workplace. What do we need an office for? It has changed the way we look at the workplace—as collaboration and ideation spaces, and a physical setting to build social capital. Why do we need so many layers of management? It has loosened the corporate hierarchy and made us think of ways to organize ourselves differently. It has given rise to WFA—'work from anywhere'. Do we need this meeting? Do I have to visit her office? Can't these meetings be virtual or perhaps done differently? Isn't it important to look at an employee's holistic wellness? Of course, the well-being of people, especially their mental and emotional well-being, is crucial. The list goes on. We are seeing revolutionary changes in the offing, much like the paradigm shifts the industrial age or the Internet revolution brought about.

While the pandemic has heralded some new changes, it has also accelerated many that were slowly gaining speed and traction. Technology, world order, people's attitudes—they are all changing and have been given a kick by the pandemic. It's this heady mixture that will redefine how we work. Let's just explore these changes in some details—as they say, understanding the context is half the way to the solution!

In August 2017, Credit Suisse analysts reported that the disruptive force of technology was killing older companies at a much faster rate than the way it was decades ago, and squeezing employees, investors and other stakeholders. 'The average age of a company listed on the S&P 500 [Standard and Poor's 500] has fallen from almost 60 years in the 1950s to less than 20 years currently,' the report stated, adding that automation was the number one 'disruptive force'.[1]

Moreover, research findings from Innosight, a US-based consultancy, shows a dramatic decline in the average company lifespan since 1980.[2] By 2027, the average age of companies on the S&P 500 could be 12 years, down from around 35 in 1980! So what is causing this churn and this rate of change?

In the course of the next decade, we are going to see many forces impacting organizations, some of them catalysed by the pandemic. It has let loose a whole host of changes, primarily about how we work and where we work. A caveat: we all know that predicting the future is fraught with the risk that the exercise may not be accurate, and I am not a futurist in any sense. However, it helps to understand the probable contours of the future to know its potential impact on organizations and HR.

Here are some major trends that could impact the future organizations.

AI and Automation

Automation will have a significant influence on organizations, as many routine jobs could possibly be eliminated. A McKinsey report on 'Technology, Jobs, and the Future of Work' outlines that about 60 per cent of all occupations have at least 30 per cent activities that are technically automatable, based on currently demonstrated technologies.[3] Watch out, many of us will be doing a somewhat different job in the next few years!

The pandemic has also accelerated the digitization of many processes—every business will move to become fully digital. Moreover, Artificial Intelligence (AI) will have a bigger impact in augmenting decision-making in some jobs, making the task more data-based and real time. Thus, freeing up managerial time and attention and allowing for focus on different and more impactful tasks. However, this is easier said than done. Research shows that a successful adoption of these AI technologies will need a thoughtful, human-centric approach. The march of the mobile phone, powered by mobile supercomputing, will continue, leading to the 'wearables revolution'. We need to prepare for the huge impact technology will have on business, jobs and people.[4]

Smart Offices and Hybrid Remote-Working

The Internet of Things (IoT) and virtual working technologies will definitely make our offices smarter, even if our homes and cities take more time to be so. Offices will now be 'phygital' as the difference between the physical and the digital will get blurred. During the current pandemic, we have seen that organizations and people have taken to remote-working—many things that we never thought possible are now clearly feasible. Offices will transform into hubs for collaboration, team brainstorming and team forming activities. I believe we will probably see a lot more of the hybrid remote working model in many sectors, with the extent of remote working ranging from 10–50 per cent depending upon the industry and nature of work.[5] Supported by other technologies like virtual reality (VR) and augmented reality (AR), the applications for businesses will be far-reaching, particularly in our workplace, creating a truly phygital environment. This is clearly a big area for organizations to consciously leverage—enabling greater productivity, collaboration and security. Welcome to the world of 'anywhere employee'!

Sustainable Environmental Action

Sustainability and environmental protection will continue to become a bigger driver for change across organizations. The whole ecosystem of clean energy will grow exponentially, impacting business as we know it today. Climate change will demand more urgent attention in the corporate world. We have seen organizations like Unilever that have made 'sustainability' their core purpose. This pandemic has also made organizations take a deeper look at the social impact they are creating. As the focus on Environment, Social and (Corporate) Governance (ESG) grows, organizations will need to rethink how they are being socially/environmentally conscious and sustainable.

These trends are all in the context of global geo-politics—protectionism, regulations and other related areas, and they will all impact businesses and how we see HR. The predictions are that GDP growth over the next decade or so will be led by the quality of talent and not just by an increase in talent supply. Further, we can see that jobs in service-based industries will grow globally, over goods-producing industries. The pandemic could influence global organizations to de-risk their supply chains, which could lead to an increase in manufacturing in India. Putting these together, it is likely that growth in India will be spurred only by the right quality of talent and unless our education system rises up to the skills challenge, we could have a large number of unemployable people, leading to increasing inequality and social tensions.

Let us now look at the likely changes in the attitudes of people over the next decade. As we all go through this pandemic, some of our behaviours and attitudes would change significantly. This is a dynamic process, and the changes could be fast and furious. In fact, one of the key focus areas for HR could be to monitor these attitudes regularly, so that we tailor our HR offerings appropriately. Here are a few trends that we could see in people and their attitudes:

1. **New career paradigm:** When I ask fresh engineering or management graduates who enter the corporate world about how they envision their careers, I find that they look at a horizon of about three to four years; no one says that they want to be the CEO of a company and retire. Given the various changes in the job environment, one can surmise that people will be forced to plan for shorter career horizons. Tenures in organizations will be shorter, unless the organizations provide opportunities for talent to reinvent and re-skill themselves. Equally, people are living longer and the population is getting older. With longer working lives and fast-changing businesses, we will probably see people reinvent their careers over their working life and make a couple of significant pivots. While 'standardization' was the default mode for large organizations previously, there is now a move towards greater customization. However, to do that, they need to invest significantly in learning. There will be a greater focus on developing skills and less on formal education degrees, thus, leading to a new 'skills economy'. Therefore, this focus on relevant skills and shorter career horizons will require people to develop multiple deep skills over time.

2. **Flexibility and gig-working:** There will be an increasing demand for flexibility as the work-life balance becomes critically important to people. With remote working getting a big boost during the pandemic, we will see more people opting to do 'gig work' as an extension of this desire for flexibility. With the advent of phygital workplaces and hybrid remote working, there will be more opportunities for enhancing flexibility of work and the workforce. There are already many organizations like Swiggy, Ola, Zomato, Uber and Dunzo which primarily work with 'gig workers'. Alternate talent pools will open up for organizations that are willing to tap into this trend—location-agnostic talent, part-time home workers, people with disabilities, etc. People who had given up their careers to be caregivers may now get back into some form of part-time working. With increasing gig working, short career tenures and a focus on specific skill/specialism, we would perhaps see newer forms of employee collectives taking root. Communities of practice, interest groups and skill guilds could be some examples.
3. **Multigenerational workforce:** The diversity of our workforce will increase and we will have a number of very different 'personas' working together. There will also be a higher drive for people to express their individuality. Talent from the interiors of the country, from different backgrounds and across generations will join the workforce in increasing numbers. A CEO recently told me that he received three types of mail from his employees. One starts with 'Dear Sir', the other with 'Dear Mr Iyer' and yet another with 'Hi Deepak'. Unlike in the past, there is now a desire to express the

varied desires and attitudes of such diverse groups. Tapping into diversity will become more of a business priority as it will have a direct link to the performance of the organization, the engagement of its employees and the innovativeness of the business establishment.

4. **Desire for change:** The younger generation joining the workforce will be increasingly focused on the impact they make in the world. They would also like their organizations to be more socially conscious, sustainable and have a larger purpose. Why do I say that? Just look at the number of young people on social media, making their point of view known on many issues. With increased awareness of issues, a greater opportunity to voice their ideas and spurred by a deep-seated desire to see change, the younger generation is keen to make a purposeful impact. Some investors, activist groups and other stakeholders would also push for a focus on sustainability. We already saw that during the Business Roundtable in 2019, 181 global CEOs committed greater focus on stakeholders rather than on the shareholders, with an emphasis on environment, society, etc.[6] Moreover, people will look for more meaningful jobs, ones that they find purposeful. The pandemic and remote working have also 'loosened' our hierarchies, and this expectation might continue. Employee collectives may come together for issues that question the business actions of their organizations if they go against their social focus. Recent examples in the United States (US) with Google are a pointer to such trends.
5. **Stress and mental health issues:** Rapidly evolving technologies and a fast-changing society will further alienate the workforce, resulting in increasing mental

health issues and stress, with the cost of these being significant to business. Increasing screen use, need for multitasking and social pressures could point to more stressful lives. The pandemic has also brought to the fore issues of employee health and holistic well-being. With the social connection of office disappearing, emotional and mental well-being, in particular, will take centre-stage as employees constantly search for meaning in the work that they do. Organizations will have to think of a holistic well-being approach.

The impact of these changes will vary with industries. For instance, the media and entertainment sector will see significantly more changes than, say, the mining industry. But it is useful to step back and understand what could be the lay of the land in the next decade as we think about our businesses and our people.

Key Takeaways

- Change is everywhere and it is accelerating.
- The longevity of large corporations is under question; they need to renew and reinvent to stay relevant.
- There are a few megatrends that will affect all industries—the impact of technology and automation, remote working, clean energy and environment action. However, there could be some other industry-specific trends.
- There are also some likely changes in people demographics, people's attitudes and needs and societal trends that we need to be cognizant of. Some of the key ones are shorter career horizons and focus on skills, greater diversity of our workforce, increase

in flexible work and gig work, increased mental health issues and the employee's interest in purpose and social impact.

Look at your industry and identify what big strategic changes could impact it in the next few years. Think of an industry that is adjacent to yours and what could be the factors that would impact it over the years. Which of those could be relevant to your industry? Look at the demographics and skills of your workforce, and think about the different archetypal 'personas' that are present. What kinds of changes do you expect in your workforce over the next few years?

References

1. Michael Sheetz, 'Technology Killing Off Corporate America: Average Life Span of Companies Under 20 Years,' *CNBC*, 24 August 2017, https://www.cnbc.com/2017/08/24/technology-killing-off-corporations-average-lifespan-of-company-under-20-years.html. Accessed on 2 September 2021.
2. S. Patrick Viguerie, Ned Calder and Brian Hindo, '2021 Corporate Longevity Forecast,' Innosight, May 2021, https://www.innosight.com/insight/creative-destruction/. Accessed on 2 September 2021.
3. Michael Chui, James Manyika and Mehdi Miremadi, 'Four Fundamentals of Workplace Automation,' McKinsey, 1 November 2015, www.mckinsey.com. Accessed on 2 September 2021.
4. James Manyika, 'Technology, Jobs, and the Future of Work,' McKinsey, 24 May 2017, https://www.mckinsey.com/featured-insights/employment-and-growth/technology-jobs-and-the-future-of-work. Accessed on 2 September 2021.

5. Aaron De Smet, Bonnie Dowling, Mihir Mysore and Angelika Reichhttps, 'It's Time for Leaders to Get Real about Hybrid', McKinsey, 9 July 2021, https://www.mckinsey.com/business-functions/people-and-organizational-performance/our-insights/its-time-for-leaders-to-get-real-about-hybrid. Accessed on 20 October 2021.
6. 'One Year Later: Purpose of a Corporation,' Business Roundtable, 19 August 2019, https://purpose.businessroundtable.org/. Accessed on 2 September 2021.

2

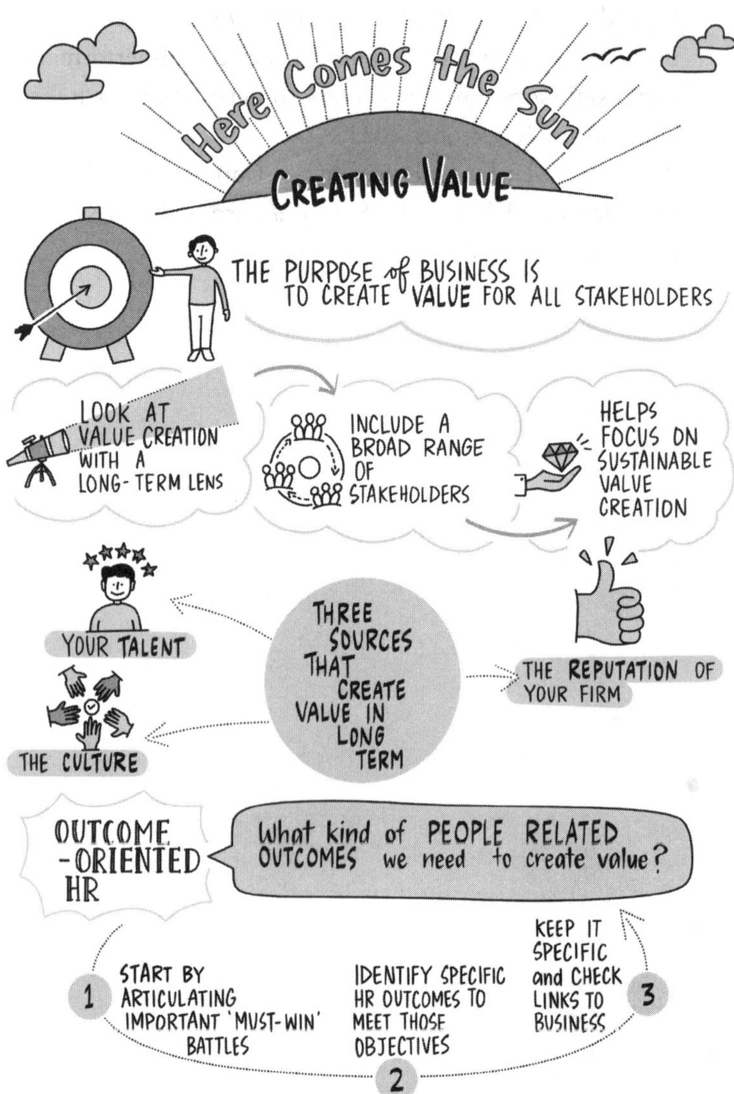
Here Comes the Sun
CREATING VALUE
THE PURPOSE of BUSINESS IS TO CREATE VALUE FOR ALL STAKEHOLDERS
LOOK AT VALUE CREATION WITH A LONG-TERM LENS
INCLUDE A BROAD RANGE OF STAKEHOLDERS
HELPS FOCUS ON SUSTAINABLE VALUE CREATION
THREE SOURCES THAT CREATE VALUE IN LONG TERM
YOUR TALENT
THE CULTURE
THE REPUTATION OF YOUR FIRM
OUTCOME-ORIENTED HR
What kind of PEOPLE RELATED OUTCOMES we need to create value?
1
START BY ARTICULATING IMPORTANT 'MUST-WIN' BATTLES
2
IDENTIFY SPECIFIC HR OUTCOMES TO MEET THOSE OBJECTIVES
3
KEEP IT SPECIFIC and CHECK LINKS TO BUSINESS

Over the years, I found that we in HR have an existential problem! Is HR really needed? Is it valued? These doubts come up every now and then. If you are an HR executive in India and especially if you are middle aged, you would recollect the many discussions of getting HR 'at the top table'. There will be a strident group which will emphatically state that unless HR understands and talks the language of business, it will not be at the top table. And an equally vociferous group will aver that the role of HR is to champion the cause of people, otherwise left on its own, businesses will not focus on people. Sounds familiar? However, in the recent past I sensed a little bit of equanimity amongst the HR fraternity. We seem to have realized that there is a seat at the top table for the 'people function' (as HR is also known), if it can help create value. This chapter is a quick reminder of what that is all about.

Let's start with the premise that the purpose of a business is to create value for all stakeholders—its customers, employees, suppliers, shareholders and the society it works in.

Every successful business has to create something of value. It probably starts with what value you are giving to your customers or clients. That leads to value creation for all other stakeholders. The tagline or motto for Y Combinator, a startup incubator founded by Paul Graham, is 'Make something people want'. There's nothing more valuable than an unmet need that is just becoming fixable. Focus on what is it that you can do to make life easier or better for someone—that leads to value.

But over time, many organizations, driven by market expectations, tend to put greater weight on the value they are creating for shareholders, as opposed to all other stakeholders. This needs reframing on two vectors. First, organizations could expand the focus of value creation to include a broad range of stakeholders, not just shareholders. And second, look at value creation in the long term; that will bring a broader focus than one on today's profits and share price. As a 2020 McKinsey report pointed out, short-termism is a major issue in today's organizations, and a long-term view of all stakeholders is essential.[1] A greater focus on ESG goals is the way forward. Take, for instance, Unilever. Their focus on sustainability and their transparency in updating progress on their ESG goals has been seen as the gold standard.[2] Oil companies like BP are also committing to greater clean energy goals.[3] There is a movement by the big funds to also invest in companies that focus on sustainable value creation over a longer period. Tata is a great example of organizations that prioritize long-term value creation across all stakeholder groups. I have had the privilege of working with Infosys that has also been at the forefront of emphasizing ESG goals.[4]

Clearly, if we drop focus on the value to our customers or clients, we will soon lose revenue and profits, and thus, value to shareholders. Similarly, if we don't provide value to employees, they will leave. Moreover, we may not be able to attract the right talent we need. While there may be some lag in its impact on profits, it will certainly come. However, in service businesses, this impact could be seen faster.

Even if you are not the CEO of a company but are heading a business unit, try and look at a three-year plan for your unit. What would your goals be and what would it take you to reach those in that time? This perspective, over a longer period, helps in sustainable value creation at any level.

Let's now look at an alternate perspective—flip the focus on the sources of value. When we look at the sources that create value, the traditional ones are capital, brand, access to raw materials, distribution, etc. However, those are replicable and not sustainable in the long term. From my perspective, the three sustainable sources of value are Talent (people and their capabilities), Culture (behaviours) in the organization and Reputation (brand) of the firm. They all take time to build, are not easily replicable and are the true sources of sustainable value creation. Do you agree?

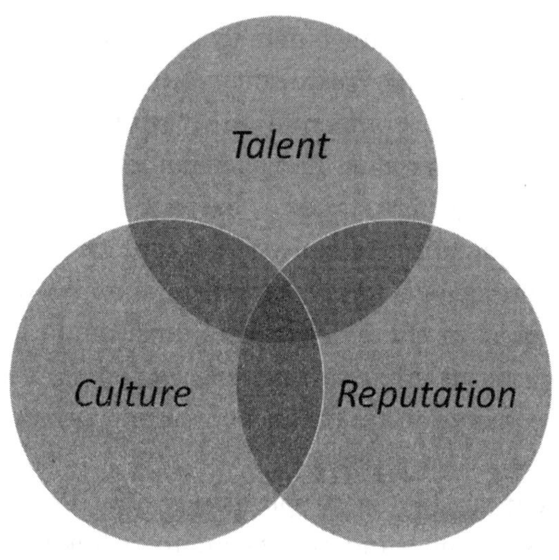

The Three Sustainable Sources of Value

In a world where change and disruption are going to be the order of the day, assets or property will not be sustainable sources of value to the organization. If you have the right talent exhibiting the right behaviours, you can thrive in change.

Value in organizations is created by a series of initiatives and actions linked to the strategy of the organization—a series of 'jobs to be done' that realize value. These jobs to be done need the right talent, capabilities, behaviours and systems, all appropriately integrated together in the business. That is the core role of the people function in creating value.

Result-Oriented Framework

Our traditional human resource management systems approach people issues through a silo functional lens. The early books on personnel management by Edwin Flippo[5] referred to areas like recruitment and selection, training and development, compensation, performance appraisal, etc. Over time, personnel management gave way to human resource management, and a broader terminology took over—talent acquisition, talent development, performance management, leadership development and so on. But we still look at it in silos. While this functional classification is good in terms of assessing knowledge or competency, this perspective and approach may seem narrow when we attempt to solve business issues.

In recent times, the people issues have been becoming increasingly complex and have begun to be linked to different aspects of the business. For instance, it is not how we can improve the selection process of a particular firm, but how that links to the type of talent being hired, the talent mix, the roles for which they are being hired, the business impact of those roles, the profile of hiring managers, etc. So things are getting more nuanced and deeply intertwined with key business considerations.

In my conversations with various business leaders, I have realized that there is a crying need for a more holistic approach to people issues and a sharper focus on outcomes. CEOs have questions like, 'How can I get a competitive people cost structure in my business?' and not questions like 'What training programme is needed?' They want answers to key business issues. Moreover, when I speak to CEOs and CHROs of start-ups, the constant refrain I hear is that they would like HR to be 'no nonsense, no bullshit' and link everything to business needs. Their mantra is 'do whatever makes business sense, but execute immediately'. This led me to think deeply about how we approach issues in the HR function and deliberate on a better way.

Many years ago, when I was with Unilever, based out of Singapore, I had attended a session by the late Dr Clayton Christensen, the Kim B. Clark professor of business administration at Harvard Business School and guru of 'disruptive innovation'. He spoke about strawberry milkshake. A fast food chain, interested in improving milkshake sales, spent months doing market research, peppering customers with questions about their milkshakes: 'Is it thick enough?' 'What are right flavours?' This milkshake was primarily targeted at children who would come back from school in the afternoon and in the evening.[6]

But they were surprised to find that quite a few milkshakes were being sold in the morning. Why was it selling more in the morning and not in the afternoon, unlike what they had anticipated? After conducting in-depth interviews, the team discovered that customers were buying the milkshakes for breakfast during their morning commute. Instead of caring about thickness or flavour, customers were actually drawn to the fact that it was easier to drink in a car on the way to work and could stave off hunger until lunch. In this instance, the competitor wasn't other milkshakes, but easy to eat breakfast foods like bagels or bananas. So, what did the customers need in the morning? They wanted something filling, healthy and easy to carry and keep as they drove to work. That's the insight. If we identify what problem the customer wants to get solved, we come with a workable solution. In fact, it is the core of design thinking.

Let us now apply it to the people function. Instead of looking at functional actions, let's look at the key business and people problems that you, as a business leader or an HR leader, would like to solve. Given your overall business objectives, what people-related outcomes are needed to successfully meet those objectives? What jobs do you want done in your business to meet your overall strategic objectives?

That's the 'outcome-oriented' framework we are talking about, something that we could use more of in our businesses.

As a leader, here is how you can approach this in a few simple steps.

1. Ask yourself: 'What are the top strategic objectives of your business? What outcomes do you want to drive in your business?' These are your 'Must-Win Battles' in the market (for those who like competitive metaphors).
2. Think about what people-related outcomes you need in place to get those overall business objectives.
3. Describe those 'people outcomes' more specifically and then work out the set of actions that will enable that outcome.

Let's take an example. Here is the case of a consumer durables company that makes products for use in the kitchen (like mixers, toasters, blenders), home (air purifiers, irons), men's grooming (trimmers, shavers), beauty care (hair straighteners), etc. A large range of products are sold through traditional retail trade, a significant part through chain stores and modern trade and also through a growing e-commerce channel. There is competition from low-cost players, but this company has built a strong brand and is known for good quality. Thus, a key lever for the growth of this company would be innovation—new products that meet the needs of a changing population.

So what could be the **strategic outcomes** (or Must-Win Battles) for the business? Probably these three:

1. Revenue from new products to grow over the next three years.
2. Differentiate through services.
3. Drive cost competitiveness in basic products.

Given these strategic outcomes, what could be the people-related outcomes or jobs that you would need done that will help achieve these strategic outcomes? These could be:

1. Ensure that you have the right culture for end-to-end innovation.
2. Implement the right organization structure to drive innovation in products and 'go to market' approaches.
3. Ensure that you have the right talent for the delivering your strategic priorities and that they work effectively to achieve your objectives.

We then define these people outcomes a bit more sharply and move on to various actions to achieve those outcomes. First, make the outcomes specific to the strategic deliverable of the business. So the question we have to ask is, 'If this people outcome is not done, can I achieve my business goal?' We are looking for a unequivocal 'no' as an answer. Second, make it as sharply defined and measurable as possible.

Frankly, this is not rocket science. It is just disciplined thinking in terms of detailing specific outcomes we would like to see or jobs we would like to get done. From my experience, this is an area where leaders could invest more time to clearly articulate the people outcomes needed to achieve the business outcomes they have outlined. These people outcomes could be in areas of talent, culture, engagement, systems, etc. All it needs is for the leadership team to come together, discuss and clearly articulate what is needed in a people-related outcome. That helps get sharper focus on what we need to do.

Just to get you started, I have identified a set of the key outcomes that are needed by organizations to create value. These outcomes or jobs to be done are foundational—essential to drive business, build competitive advantage and help create value.

I have identified 10 Foundational Outcomes as follows:

- Foundational Outcome 1: Create an architecture of inclusive, fair and equitable processes.
- Foundational Outcome 2: Ensure you have a competitive cost structure.
- Foundational Outcome 3: Attract and engage the right talent, and ensure that you have right talent for the right jobs at the right time.

- Foundational Outcome 4: Ensure the business achieves the results as planned and expected.
- Foundational Outcome 5: Drive the right behaviours needed to win and create value.
- Foundational Outcome 6: Ensure you have the right leaders to drive the business and a pipeline of leaders ready for succession.
- Foundational Outcome 7: Provide opportunities for every employee to learn and grow.
- Foundational Outcome 8: Get the workforce fully engaged and motivated for giving their best.
- Foundational Outcome 9: Build a diverse, multigenerational workforce.
- Foundational Outcome 10: Ensure that the organization has a larger purpose and employees feel purposeful and realize their potential.

These are generic people-related outcomes that can probably cover most of a business's key needs.

However, there could be other outcomes too; this is not an exhaustive list. But this is to give you an idea of how we can think through our people-related actions without getting siloed and with a focus on the outcome.

As we go further in this book, the focus will be on how we can look at each of these people outcomes to maximize the potential of people, culture and reputation as key drivers of value creation.

Shiv Shivakumar, group executive president, corporate strategy and business development, Aditya Birla Group, and former chairman and CEO of PepsiCo India, has this perspective:

A company has many assets—tangible and intangible. The most important asset of any company is its people and the culture that binds them together to produce extraordinary results. People and culture are both tangible at one level, i.e. you can check the capability of people, the responsiveness of a culture, etc. They are also intangible at another level.

They are intangible because people today are of the mindset that they volunteer their time to an organization and are not employees. The average life span of a company was 60 years in 1958. Today the average life span of a company is less than 20 years.[7] The individual had in the '60s a 'join and retire mentality' and spent 25–30 years in one organization. Those days are over. Today, the person is willing to give a company two to three years and then check his learnings and benefit. In a sense, there are no permanent companies and no permanent employees. Today, the employee's dreams are far bigger than the company vision.

Employees are volunteers at one level and ambassadors at another level. When the company purpose excites them, they give more of themselves to the company. When the company treats them fairly, they become great ambassadors for the company and one sees that reflected in Glassdoor reviews, etc.

A company needs employees to buy into the strategy and then execute it. The value generation in every company comes from this simple logic. I have a simple acronym for it: BITS-EDGE, which stands for 'Buy Into Strategy for Everyday Great Execution'.

A competitor can copy anything from us, except our culture, that's the secret sauce of value creation. The value creation journey starts with having the right people in your team:

1. People who are talented and not toxic.
2. People who are collaborative and not cynical.
3. People who have pride and not arrogance.
4. People who are good leaders and also great followers.
5. People who tell you the truth and not what they think you want to hear.
6. People who are institution builders.

I have always likened running a company to the old aircraft cockpit—a cockpit which had the pilot, co-pilot and the navigator. The pilot is the CEO, the co-pilot the CFO and the navigator is the HR person, showing people the compass of true north. All three need each other to fly the plane!

Key Takeaways

- The purpose of business is to create value for all stakeholders. However, in reality, due to the pressure of market forces, the biggest focus tends to be on value to shareholders.
- Looking at value creation with a long-term lens and including a broader range of stakeholders helps get a focus on sustainable value creation.
- An alternate way is to look at the sources that create value. While many asset-based sources are replicable, three sources create value in the long term—your

talent, the culture or behaviours exhibited by people and the reputation of the firm.

- Outcome-oriented HR is a method that can help frame the kind of people-related outcomes you need to ensure that you create value by meeting your overall organizational goals.
- One way to define outcomes is to outline the jobs to be done to support your business goals.
- The key is to start with the business itself and articulate the strategic priorities for the business—the important 'must-win battles' for the business.
- Follow that up by articulating the HR outcomes you would need to meet those business objectives. Keep it specific and check its link to the business. 'If this is not done, will we be able to meet our overall business objective?' is the key question.

References

1. Marc Goedhart and Tim Koller, 'The Value of Value Creation', McKinsey, 16 June 2020, https://www.mckinsey.com/business-functions/strategy-and-corporate-finance/our-insights/the-value-of-value-creation. Accessed on 5 September, 2021.
2. 'Unilever Sustainable Living Plan', HUL, https://hul-performance-highlights.hul.co.in/performance-highlights-fy-2019-20/sustainable-living.php. Accessed on 3 September 2021.
3. 'Who We Are: Our Purpose', BP, https://www.bp.com/en/global/corporate/who-we-are/our-purpose.html. Accessed on 3 September 2021.
4. 'Infosys ESG Vision, 2030', Infosys, https://www.infosys.com/content/dam/infosys-web/en/about/corporate-

responsibility/esg-vision-2030/index.html. Accessed on 3 September 2021.

5. Edwin B. Flippo, *Personnel Management*, McGraw-Hill Management Series, 1984.
6. 'Jobs to Be Done', Christensen Institute, https://www.christenseninstitute.org/jobs-to-be-done/. Accessed on 3 September 2021.
7. Michael Sheetz, 'Technology Killing Off Corporate America: Average Life Span of Companies under 20 Years', *CNBC*, 24 August 2017, https://www.cnbc.com/2017/08/24/technology-killing-off-corporations-average-lifespan-of-company-under-20-years.html. Accessed on 20 October 2021.

3

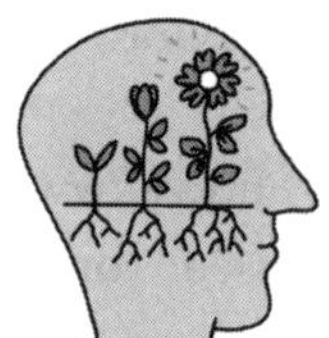

Land of Hope and Dreams

BUILDING ON NEW RESEARCH ON LEVERAGING PEOPLE POTENTIAL

THE CURRENT PARADIGM OF HR FUNCTION IS BASED ON RESOURCE-BASED PERSPECTIVE OF STRATEGY

EMOTIONS LIKE **HAPPINESS, PRIDE, COMPASSION, GRATITUDE** ARE CORE TO MANY POSITIVE BEHAVIOURS IN INDIVIDUALS and GROUPS

RESEARCH ON **HOW TO GET THE BEST OUT OF PEOPLE**

- PRINCIPLES OF **POSITIVE PSYCHOLOGY**
- UNDERSTANDING ROLE OF **EMOTIONS**
- NEUROSCIENCE OF **LEARNING AND HABIT FORMATION**
- PSYCHOLOGICAL **SAFETY**
- GROWTH **MINDSET**

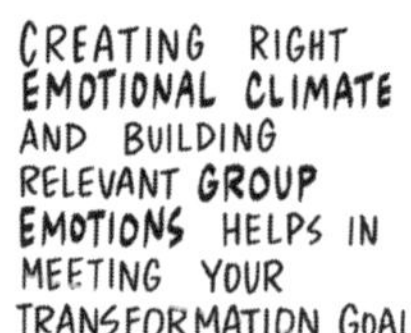

CREATING RIGHT **EMOTIONAL CLIMATE** AND BUILDING RELEVANT **GROUP EMOTIONS** HELPS IN MEETING YOUR TRANSFORMATION GOALS

'TYRANNY OF LARGE ORGANIZATIONS'— IS A BARRIER

NEED LEADERS and PEOPLE CHAMPIONS TO **BELIEVE** and MAKE THE CHANGES

CORE ROLE OF PEOPLE FUNCTION

INCLUSIVE and FAIR ORGANIZATION DESIGNER and ADVOCATE

TALENT PARTNER and COACH

CULTURE AND EMOTIONS ARCHITECT and CATALYST

While I was at Hindustan Unilever (HUL), I attended many conferences and workshops on personnel management. But in 1997, close on the heels of the merger between Hindustan Lever and Brooke Bond Lipton, I was part of an HR conference with a difference. It was called Disha, and led by the then personnel director at HUL, Ani Lahiri. Ani was a technical/manufacturing professional who had taken over the HR function and a passionate and energetic leader. For the first time in HUL, the conference was held completely outdoors, on the banks of the Ganges near Rishikesh. So, the big difference was that instead of listening to interminable speeches through the day (with overhead projector [OHP] transparencies, for those who remember it), the group had a dialogue. The discussions were centred around how we could create a new paradigm for HR. It was about our mindsets, our people philosophy and our industrial relations policies.

One could sense a strong desire amongst the group for some big changes. I recount this incident only to bring out that we have all been through this before. Every organization should go through this reflective moment once in a few years. Every few years, every business and HR team must come together to share this feeling of dissatisfaction with the present and leave with a resolve for change. As we look at the post-pandemic world, I sense that this need for change is much stronger.

And as we go through tremendous changes, perhaps it is time to step back and reflect on whether the current paradigm of human resources is appropriate and whether it needs to change. But before we get to that, let's understand how the current paradigm of human resources has evolved to be about 'strategic management'.

One of the fundamental questions in the field of strategic management is how firms achieve and sustain competitive advantage. We can look at this in four successive threads of thought. The first is the Porterian perspective of the 1980s, where the dominant paradigm was the 'Competitive Forces Approach'. Its emphasis was on industry analysis and on the actions that firms can initiate to take positions against competitive forces.[1]

This was followed by the 'strategic conflict perspective'. The approach was based on game theory (a branch of applied mathematics that deals with situations in which parties make decisions that are interdependent) and viewed competitive outcomes as a function of effectiveness through which firms keep their rivals off balance. This did not, however, help build enduring sources of competitive advantage. This was followed by models of strategy emphasizing efficiency, which was called the 'resource-based perspective'. The link between firm resources and sustained competitive advantage was examined, and four indicators of a firm's resources to generate sustained competitive advantage were identified—value, rareness, imitability and substitutability. The dominant thought was that strategic advantage could be captured through firm-level efficiency advantages, and that superior systems and structures would lead to greater profitability. The current paradigm of HR is still strongly rooted in this resource-based perspective.

Subsequently, the concept of 'dynamic capabilities' emerged. This thought has grown from the resource-based perspective, with the premise that firms have the capacity to renew capabilities, and that exploiting internal and external firm-specific competences to address changing environment would determine business success. The late C.K. Prahalad, who was the Paul and Ruth McCracken Distinguished University Professor of Strategy, Ross School of Business at the University of Michigan and a celebrated management thinker, developed 'core competencies' as an offshoot of this school of thought.[2] Much of the notions on the role of culture and how culture 'eats strategy for breakfast' stems from this perspective.

As strategy shifted to the Internet era, the focus of strategy moved to 'network effects' and the concept of an ecosystem (the 'walled garden' approach of Apple is an example)—but equally, the importance of talent has come into stronger focus. Talent is fast-emerging as a source of innovation. However, even with these new age ideas of strategy, the focus has largely been on 'talent as a resource'—for instance, when they speak of talent clusters in Silicon Valley and how the ecosystem enables innovation and entrepreneurship.

Over the last decade, there have been many new theories in the behavioural sciences. A strong thread of positive psychology has developed over the years, championed by Martin Seligman, a professor at the University of Pennsylvania and pioneer of positive psychology. Positive psychology focuses on leveraging strengths and using the power of emotions, notably optimism.[3] There is now a significant body of research talking about the 'growth mindset', led by Carol Dweck, a professor of psychology at Stanford University.[4] Amy Edmondson, professor of leadership at the Harvard Business School, highlights the preeminent role of psychological safety in team effectiveness.[5] David DeSteno, a professor of psychology at Northeastern University, demonstrates with his research that emotions of gratitude, compassion and pride help build resilience in people.[6]

Research in neuroscience has been revealing the importance of emotions—empathy, compassion, gratitude—and its effect on team effectiveness and resilience. There is a lot of literature based on purpose that has led to organizations articulating a larger purpose. In a way, all these threads of research are linked—the underlying theme being that human potential has not been leveraged appropriately. The post-pandemic world has also led to a rethink of some of our dominant assumptions on people. The need for flexibility, more autonomy and a greater focus on resilience is coming out stronger than ever.

Clearly, that's the big emerging insight. The current paradigm of management looks at people as a resource, not to be tossed around but to be developed and grown. However, contemporary research is pointing to an area in which organizations could do much more to leverage the enormous potential of their people. Jobs are very important to people. In addition to their livelihoods, jobs give people an identity and allow them to build their social networks. Given all this, why are many organizations failing to leverage their people potential?

I would suggest three reasons why organizations have not been able to maximize the human potential of every employee. First, there is something about the tyranny of large organizations. Every well-intentioned idea could meet its Waterloo in the hustle and bustle of organizational priorities. The 'quarter-on-quarter pressure' of listed companies to manage analyst and investor expectations also adds to this. But there are a few companies that seem to have worked out a way to get the very best out of people. Vineet Nayyar, as CEO of HCL, came up with this path-breaking 'employee first, customer second' philosophy.[7]

The second reason could be that all these new theories and ideas haven't been implemented well in organizations yet. Maybe some early adopters have taken to them, but perhaps a large number are still sceptical and waiting to see the 'proof of the pudding'.

And third, it could be our mindset. We don't want to deal with too much individuality and the resultant complexity. It could also be the time horizon that each manager thinks of in organizations these days; driving a change like that could be an arduous task, unless you are a promoter. It is just that we don't all have the energy to question the status quo.

I guess the reasons could be many, but in this book I will try and put forward some ideas that we can implement to make the change. The objective will be to maximize the potential of each person who is part of an organization. So, what is my recommendation?

First, establish and articulate what value creation means for your organization and, specifically, what it means for employees. We saw that the three sustainable sources of competitive advantage are talent, culture and the firm's reputation. Also, as mentioned earlier, it is critical to have a longer term horizon of at least five years. Specify the 'people vision' for your organization. What will your organization stand for, for your people? This is also more philosophical and can be described in terms of your overall intent.

R. Rajnarayan, former CHRO, Titan Company Ltd, underscores the benefits of paying attention to individuals and says, 'I have seen that the unconditional regard for people creates immense goodwill. People then go out of the way to do amazing stuff. I have seen our employees go the extra mile and do some incredible things for our customers. I think there is a strong business case, if you ever need one, for treating people well.' As you can see here, he talks about a culture of positive regard and respect for people in the organization, and a willingness to back them and look at people costs as a long-term investment. There are legendary stories at Titan of sales employees going out of their way to be personal friends of customers and going the extra mile. There have been instances of employees calling to check on some customers during the COVID-19 pandemic and in one case, an employee even going to the extent of helping a customer with their hospital admission. That's just an example of the people philosophy of an organization.

Second, start looking at people processes without the traditional silos. The future calls for very agile and adaptive organizations, ones that sense the environment regularly and respond to changes swiftly. These principles should be at the core of all your people processes. While some start-ups are good at this, many large organizations also became very agile during the pandemic. If you are working in a start-up, you have the advantage of not being tied to legacy processes, which can help you think through issues based on first principles. However, since there are so many things to do and the pressure and intensity are high, you would need to prioritize and keep a sharper filter for your initiatives to meet your business needs.

Third, while it could be considered only cosmetic, I would recommend we change the name of the HR function. You could call it the 'people and culture function' or, if you want to be more adventurous, call it the 'human potential maximization function'. I prefer the edgier human potential maximization. 'Why is this cosmetic name change important?' you might wonder. It could help signal that the organization is serious about people and their potential. It helps put some stakes on the ground and challenges us to achieve those. You could try this right away!

As we go further in this book, we will work on some steps you can take to maximize your people potential by focusing on relevant outcomes. However, before we jump into that, it is important to step back and rethink the key of 'Human Resources' or the people function.

◆

Nitin Paranjpe, chief operating officer (COO), Unilever PLC:

I have always wondered how the same people, with the same resources, did unbelievable things when they were chasing a ridiculous goal. I believe our fear of failure prevents us from imagining what can be done, and we underachieve to our potential.

Let me give you an example. In 2008, when I was the CEO of HUL, we were struggling as a business. One of the ideas that I toyed with was to set audacious goals. We said we would plan to add 500,000 outlets in a year—a drastic increase from the previous five years' average of adding 20,000 outlets per year. This was a wild mismatch between our ambition and our resources. If I had set 50,000 outlets as the target, we would have had negotiations and then settled for something around 30,000–35,000 outlets! But with 500,000, we were all out of scale and even out of bounds of any negotiation! We embraced this audacious goal and in six months we saw the teams break through (what we had thought were) obstacles.

I saw completely new behaviours and collaboration; the whole company was galvanized. They went for it on a best effort basis, as they were not expected to hit the target! Instead of the fear of failure, we saw different emotions. People were looking at the zone of possibilities, and we saw everyone at their best. They would have been heroes even if they hit 100,000 outlets! We eventually hit the magic number, but more importantly, we took the task of repeating it the next year and succeeded in adding 600,000 outlets!

We are normally enveloped in the fear of failure so we set moderate goals, experience negative emotions, and work without knowing the depth of capability within us. How do we change this paradigm and get everyone to maximize their potential and be at their best? In my experience, these three actions help:

1. Have a vision that is collectively inspiring but individually relatable. Each person should know what it means for them.
2. Create conditions where everyone can be a hero. Therefore, set goals that give people a chance to do heroic things, that is, our aspiration (A) should be greater than the resources (R). A > R! This enables us to explore the full depth of our capability.
3. Provide psychological safety. People should happily move out of their comfort zone without any fear of failure.

This is the new paradigm of people management we should aim for—from the fear of failure and scratching the surface of capability, to the joy of success and getting everyone to maximize their potential and be a hero!

◆

The Humane Quotient

Over the years, I have been looking for a better construct of the role of HR that puts people at the heart, recognizing their emotions. We saw earlier the enormous new body of work on positive psychology and neuroscience. We know that emotions have been underestimated and under-leveraged in organizations, and that some of the latest research led by Sigal Barsade, professor of management at the Wharton School, has thrown light on a number of areas where organizations can benefit from an understanding of emotions.[8] David DeSteno's recent research brings out the power of emotions. For instance, the emotions of gratitude and compassion are seen to be critical in building resilience in people and in making them think more long-term in their decisions.[9] Similarly, happiness or subjective well-being is seen as a critical emotion for sustained high performance. Sonja Lyubomirsky's research on happiness also gives clues on actions we can take to be happier.[10] Moreover, as I learnt from my own experience, it is clear that the ability to manage emotions at an organization level is critical for successful business transitions, especially as organizations and teams manage radical strategic change.

We need a new concept for HR for the future, one that integrates emotions and emotional intelligence much more. Traditional definitions of the role of HR have been very process-oriented and administrative, not focusing on the role as much. The first framework of HR from a role perspective was proposed by management guru and HR pioneer Dave Ulrich in *HR Champions*.[11] Ulrich's model described four roles of HR—administrative expert, employee champion, change catalyst and strategic partner. While that definition has helped transform HR in the current day, it has its drawbacks. First, the people function has changed significantly over the years and these roles are no longer relevant at times. For instance, with outsourcing and automation, the role of administrative expert is now obsolete. The concept of change catalyst and strategic partners have been long ingrained as part of the role, given the fast-changing business context, and have now become commonplace. Moreover, in the light of the new literature on organization and employee engagement and the future business context, the framework for a new role for HR needs review.

Based on the insights from my experience and analysis, and with the benefit of the latest research, I am proposing a new model to articulate the role of the HR/people function in any organization in the future. I think the future role of HR function would fall in the following categories:

1. **Equitable HR processes:** As a reflection of the current times, equity, inclusiveness and organizational justice are becoming critical. From my research, I found that the biggest cause of negative emotions was the obvious perception of the lack of fairness in organizational processes. Areas of diversity, gender pay gap and biases

in career growth are all gaining a lot of focus. The concept of fairness extends to creating psychological safety for people in their teams, leading to a truly inclusive organization. Therefore, the key role of HR would be to design people processes that are equitable and inclusive, and the leaders should take personal responsibility of creating a fair, just and inclusive organization that will lead to an increased sense of belonging for everyone. The following would be the key points of consideration to ensure a fair and just organization:

a. Does the organization have fair and equitable processes?
b. Does the organization make people feel included?
c. Do people feel that they have the psychological safety to learn and challenge?

I call this role the ***Inclusive Organization Designer and Advocate.***

2. **The right talent:** It involves regularly articulating and defining the skills, competencies and mindset needed for the organization to succeed in the future, and attracting, hiring and onboarding such talent. Also, putting in place a strong talent development mechanism to develop talent in line with future needs would be one of the key roles of the HR function. More importantly, there should be a focus on providing opportunities for people to find their purpose and work towards those. Engaging the right talent at the right time in the right roles is critical for the success of the organization. In line with the inclusiveness/fairness principle stated above, internal talent should have the same opportunities and means to

grow and progress with respect to external talent. The key considerations for the function in this area are:

a. What kind of talent do we need? When? In which roles?
b. How do we attract, hire and onboard them?
c. How do we develop and grow them? Are they finding opportunities to realize their purpose?
d. How do we renew and keep the talent relevant for the future?

I call this role the ***Talent Partner and Coach.***

3. **Articulating culture and collective emotions:** The people function has to help leaders create psychologically safe workplaces where employees feel free to express their emotions and try things without fear. We need to architect the environment for appropriate behaviours and emotions—what we call culture. Leaders also have to decide the kind of collective emotions they want to see in their teams, given their particular business situation, and put in place organizational routines and people practices to build those collective emotions. The right collective emotions at the right stage, supported by right leader behaviours, make a big difference to the organization's success. Organizational routines, HR practices and leaders play a big role in building those emotions and creating that culture. Ensuring that leaders also demonstrate the right behaviours to support those emotions becomes important. Therefore, a key role for the function would be establishing the right environment for right behaviours and leveraging the collective emotions of people.

The following questions would be the key to find solutions in this area:

a. What collective emotions and behaviours are needed in the business, given their context and challenges?
b. What organizational routines and people practices are needed to build those collective emotions and behaviours?
c. Is there a psychologically safe environment for people to be authentic and express their emotions?
d. How do we coach leaders to proactively manage the emotions needed in their teams?

I call this role the ***Culture & Emotions Architect and Catalyst.***

In these times of change, there is a serious need to review our paradigm of human resources. We have to acknowledge and leverage emotions of our people to achieve relevant goals. The diagram below, which I propose as a guide to all organizations in focusing their people function, captures this new framework. I believe this new focus on the function would enable it to prioritize the essentials of our contemporary times.

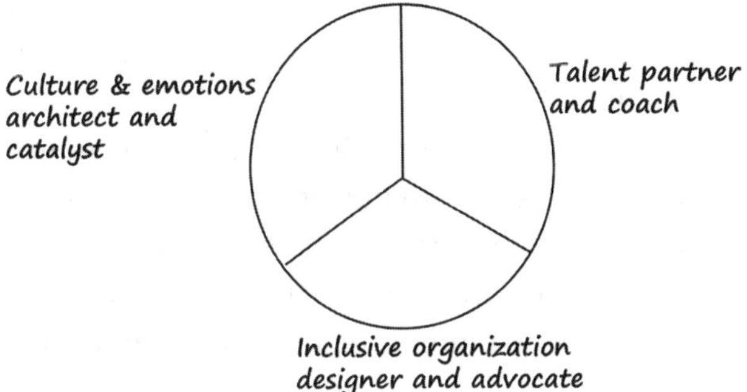

This was to give you a perspective of what could be the new focus of the HR role in any organization. Along with our strategic focus on outcomes, we will apply some of the latest insights and lots of experiences to some of the core 'jobs to be done' in any organization.

Finally, a quick word on some of the frameworks that one can use. The congruence model, developed by David Nadler and Michael Tushman in 'Competing by Design' is a good one to use.[12] The McKinsey 7S framework is a popular and useful framework that was developed by Tom Peters and Robert H. Waterman, and has stood the test of time.[13] The concept is similar to the congruence model. This framework puts a set of shared values at the heart of any organization. We then have the Hard S's—Strategy, Structure and Systems, and the Soft S's—Skills, Staff (people or talent and their capabilities) and Styles (the leadership style adopted)—all linked to each other. I found both of these to be good time-tested diagnostics to use.

Key Takeaways

- The current paradigm of human resources function has its roots in the resource-based perspective of strategy developed in the '90s, where it was considered as a resource that can lead to competitive advantage.
- However, new research in the behavioural and social sciences is giving us some new insights into how we might get the best version of people in organizations. Principles of positive psychology, a greater understanding of the role of emotions, fresh insights from neuroscience on learning and habit

formation, the work around psychological safety and growth mindset—these are some new concepts that can possibly make a difference in how we get the best out of our people.

- Specifically, emotions like happiness, pride, compassion and gratitude are seen as core to many positive behaviours, and new research has also given us insights as to how these emotions might be created in groups.
- Creating the right emotional climate and building the relevant group emotions at different stages of a business help in meeting your transformation goals. For instance, a group emotion of optimism and hope is critical as you are turning around a business and an emotion of gratitude and compassion is needed for collaboration.
- There are some possible barriers in implementing these ideas, notably, the tyranny of large organizations, the need to have leaders and people champions believe in the ideas and make the effort to bring about changes.
- To help with that, we have a new framework for thinking about the core role of the people function. There are three key roles that we should focus on:
  a. Organization designer and advocate.
  b. Talent partner and coach.
  c. Culture and emotions architect and catalyst.

  Understanding these roles will help us with the right approach to get the best version of people working in our organizations.

  The focus on people outcomes, plus the new perspective on the key roles of HR along with the application of new insights from cutting edge research will be the cornerstone to maximizing the potential of our people.

References

1. Michael E. Porter, *Competitive Advantage: Creating and Sustaining Superior Performance*, Free Press, 1998.
2. C.K. Prahalad and Gary Hamel, 'The Core Competence of the Corporation', *Harvard Business Review,* Issue: May–June 1990, https://hbr.org/1990/05/the-core-competence-of-the-corporation. Accessed on 20 October 2021.
3. Martin Seligman, *Flourish: A Visionary New Understanding of Happiness and Well-being*, Free Press, 2011.
4. Carol Dweck, *Mindset: Changing the Way You Think to Fulfil Your Potential*, Constable and Robinson, 2012.
5. Amy C. Edmondson, *The Fearless Organization: Creating Psychological Safety in the Workplace for Learning, Innovation, and Growth*, Wiley, 2018.
6. David DeSteno, *Emotional Success: The Motivational Power of Gratitude, Compassion and Pride*, Bluebird, 2018.
7. Vineet Nayyar, *Employees First, Customers Second: Turning Conventional Management Upside Down*, Harvard Business Review Press, 2010.
8. Sigal Barsade and Olivia A. O'Neill, 'Manage Your Emotional Culture,' *Harvard Business Review*, Issue: January–February 2016, https://hbr.org/2016/01/manage-your-emotional-culture. Accessed on 3 September 2021.
9. David DeSteno, *Emotional Success: The Motivational Power of Gratitude, Compassion and Pride*, Bluebird, 2018.
10. Sonja Lyubomirsky, *The How of Happiness: A New Approach to Getting the Life You Want*, Penguin, 2007.

11. Dave Ulrich, *Human Resource Champions: The Next Agenda for Adding Value and Delivering Results*, Harvard Business Review Press, 1996.
12. David A. Nadler and Michael L. Tushman, *Competing by Design: The Power of Organizational Architecture*, Oxford University Press, 1997.
13. MindTools Content Team, 'The McKinsey 7S Framework: Making Every Part of Your Organization Work in Harmony,' https://www.mindtools.com/pages/article/newSTR_91.htm. Accessed on 3 September, 2021.

4

Peaceful Easy Feeling

BUILDING FAIR AND EQUITABLE PROCESSES

THE FOUNDATION OF ANY ORGANIZATION

FAIR and INCLUSIVE PRACTICES

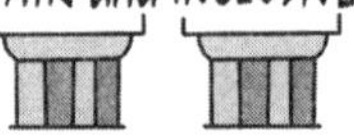

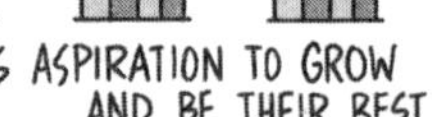

ENABLES ASPIRATION TO GROW AND BE THEIR BEST

THREE STEPS TO INCLUSION

1. ENSURE COMPLIANCE WITH REGULATIONS
2. KNOW WHAT PEOPLE EXPECT AND TAKE CARE OF THOSE
3. ASK, 'WILL THIS MAKE US WHAT WE WANT TO BE?'

THREE STEPS FOR FAIRNESS IN ORGANIZATIONS

DISTRIBUTIVE JUSTICE

RIGHT OUTCOMES/DECISIONS ARE DELIVERED

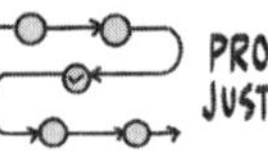

PROCEDURAL JUSTICE

THE PROCESS IS SEEN AS FAIR, CONSISTENT

INTERACTIONAL JUSTICE

DIGNITY OF INDIVIDUAL UPHELD IN ALL INTERACTIONS

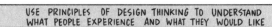

USE PRINCIPLES OF DESIGN THINKING TO UNDERSTAND WHAT PEOPLE EXPERIENCE AND WHAT THEY WOULD LIKE

TO MAKE A DIFFERENCE

START WITH TONE AT THE TOP ROLE MODELING

REARCHITECT SYSTEMS and PRACTICES (USE DATA ANALYTICS TO ELIMINATE BIAS

TRAIN and SENSITIZE MANAGERS

TRANSPARENT MEASUREMENT and REPORTING

So, here we are. We are looking at creating a truly foundational people outcome—one that every organization needs to get right. This is about creating an architecture of inclusive, fair and equitable processes.

Think of a problem or a grievance that an employee may have brought to you in the last month or so. What was the main reason for the concern? I bet you it would have ended with the employee saying, 'This is not fair'. The single biggest cause of employee discontent is perceived unfairness. Unfair pay, unfair promotions—'Why him and why not me?' Every employee wants a fair and a level playing field. A perceived lack of fairness could drain the energy and motivation of people, and lead to a dysfunctional organization. Taking this a step further, being equitable means that we recognize that different people have different needs and become committed to giving them what they need to succeed.

The foundation of any organization is based on transparent and fair practices. While many large organizations that have been in existence for a long time have established good processes, there are always gaps that one discovers. With more awareness of issues and changing attitudes, some new areas could come up. Take gender pay parity, for instance. It is a very clear focus area now though it may not have been an important issue in the past. Similarly, LGBTQ rights, bullying in the workplace and psychological safety in teams are all areas of increasingly heightened sensitivity. Organizations have to constantly review the environment, listen to employee needs and update their policies. We need to provide all employees with contextually equitable access to opportunities.

But we also need to move a step ahead of fairness. That is being inclusive. Fairness and equity lead to a feeling of inclusion. And people are now talking of 'belonging' as a step beyond inclusiveness.

I can't stress enough why a perception of equity and inclusiveness is important. It sets the base for the culture of the organization. It helps people believe in the organization and that they can meet their aspirations there. It helps build trust with others and builds collaboration. A feeling of inclusion as a member is the first stage in creating psychological safety in teams. Lastly, and most importantly, it is the right thing to do—as a humanitarian value, and as well as a principle of natural justice.

What Is the Science behind This?

There are three broad layers to examine as we look at the concept of fairness and inclusion in organizations, as in the figure below:

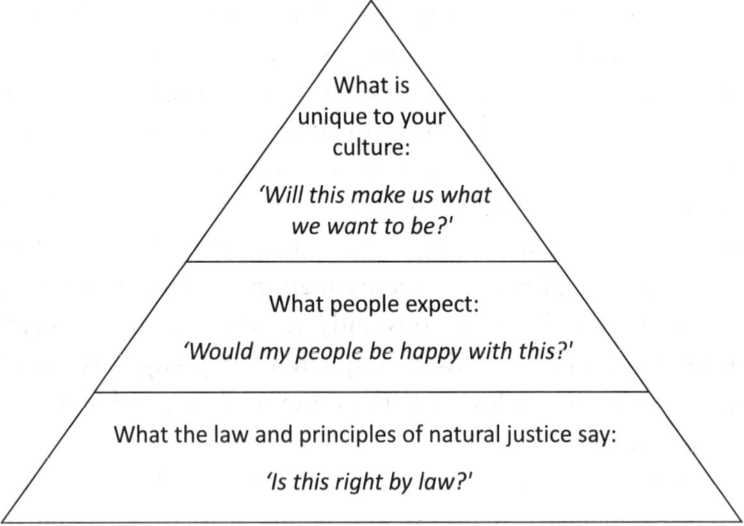
What is
unique to your
culture:
'Will this make us what
we want to be?'
What people expect:
'Would my people be happy with this?'
What the law and principles of natural justice say:
'Is this right by law?'

Of course, we need to start with what the law prescribes and the context of principles of natural justice. In addition to employment laws, one needs to consider the Companies Act, data privacy regulations, Prevention of Sexual Harassment Act, affirmative action regulations, etc. Many European countries have come up with regulations for transparency of gender pay parity.

When we look at the second group of what is 'right' by people, I introduce the concept of organizational justice, developed by psychologists Jerald Greenberg[1] and Zinta S. Byrne and Russell Cropanzano.[2]

Organizational justice is derived from equity theory, proposed by John Adams in the late '60s.[3] Adams suggested that employees try to maintain a balance between what they give to an organization against what they receive and base satisfaction with their own balance on perceptions of the same balance in colleagues. Equity theory is based on a principle that peoples' actions and motivations are guided by fairness and that discrepancies in this fairness in the workplace will spur them to try and redress it.

The three key elements of organizational justice are as follows:

1. Distributive justice refers to the perceived fairness of decision outcomes and is judged by measuring whether outcomes stick to expectations and follow a consistent principle.
2. Procedural justice is the perceived fairness of decision-making procedures and is judged by gauging whether procedures are accurate, consistent, unbiased, correctable and open to employee input. So in summary, not only must justice be done, it should also appear to have been done! Research

shows that people may accept a decision that they don't necessarily like if we have procedural justice where the process is seen as neutral and transparent, with clear decision criteria and employees participate by voicing their opinions and views.

3. Interactional justice refers to the perceived fairness of the interaction with the authority figure in implementation of procedures and distribution of justice. While there is a school of thought that interactional justice is a part of procedural justice, it is equally clear that individuals perceive the organization though interaction with bosses, who are authority figures in the organization, and place a great weight on that interaction. Therefore, it is critical we ensure that our processes uphold the dignity of the individual.

Going back to our hierarchy of elements to ensure a fair workplace, the last part deals with the culture and values of the organization. For instance, if one of the elements of your culture is meritocracy or a high performance work ethic, you need to ensure that you are transparent about what constitutes high performance, how to measure it, how to set goals and stick to them.

Diagnosis and Action

After the overview of what it means to build a fair and transparent organization, let us put together our minds on how we can make it come alive in the organization.

Try these few steps to ensure fairness and transparency.

The first step is to comply with the legal imperatives: what systems and processes do you need to ensure fairness as per the regulations? Ensure that any processes that are to be established, or any information that is needed to be displayed or communicated by these regulations are done.

Find out what your employees feel: a kind of a design thinking exercise to understand employee perceptions at key moments is usually very insightful. Unfairness normally raises its head when there is a power equation involved; for instance, in a boss-subordinate relationship, more so where the employee feels his or her choices are limited. Similarly, situations that involve a choice between two or more individuals for a benefit, like a promotion, raise or a bonus, are also potential areas where unfairness may be perceived. That's where procedural justice comes into play. Understand 'social identity'—the labels that people use to categorize or identify themselves and/or others as members of specific groups. Examine all the various 'identity groups'—do they feel valued? What could be the possible biases against them? It is recommended to have regular focus group discussions with employees to find potential red flags. The best way is to institutionalize this aspect of getting employee input—you would have your normal employee satisfaction survey or pulse survey, but it is good to create various groups of employees as 'employee experience' champions whose role is to get together regularly and highlight areas which can be improved.

Lastly, set up a robust complaint or voice mechanism that individuals can reach out to without fear. Another technique that we can adopt is some kind of organizational network analysis and see if there are more opportunities to provide equitable access to some people.

Do an audit of various employee touchpoints. One good practice many companies adopt is to map out all the employee touchpoints where decisions are being made on employees—so-called moments of truth—for fairness and inclusiveness. The question we should be asking ourselves is, 'What would you like if you were in the employees' shoes?' For instance, raises given to people in a department. While we trust and empower a manager to do the right thing, there is always a chance that some sort of favouritism may creep in. Encouraging managers to be honest by training them to take data-based decisions and giving them right data at the right time helps. This is where technology and analytics can help in a big way. Helping them before a decision with the right data and also showing the trend of decision-making helps identify issues. Research shows that well-designed algorithms can help managers make better decisions—it gives them that nudge to think and reflect, even if the final decision is fully theirs. Other practices like 'pre-mortem', where the possibilities of what could go wrong are discussed, help in bringing more fairness and thoughtfulness into decisions.

This is a tough balance the organization must strike—to what extent would you empower your people manager to take decisions? I guess this depends on the quality of your people managers. It could also vary by industry; large scale industry employers will not always be able to ensure the right quality of managers. Hence, they might have to put in other controls. A couple of ways to control these are by using teams of managers to look at exceptional cases and ensuring there is enough data to make those decisions in a fair manner or have a mechanism to review the justifications of managers for taking certain decisions. In Infosys, anyone aggrieved can raise a Hearing Employees and Resolve (HEAR) query. Once the team gets the complaint, they look at the severity of the case. In cases where it concerns the treatment by their manager or performance management, they constitute a panel of a couple of senior managers from another unit and HR. This panel looks at data and speaks to people independently, and gives a decision that is binding on all employees. The panel regularly checks how many of these decisions from the HEAR panel go in favour of the employee and if it is reasonably significant, then it is considered to be on the right track.

There is a very interesting difference between bias and noise that Daniel Kahneman, Eugene Higgins professor of psychology, emeritus, Princeton University, and his co-authors talk about in *Noise: A Flaw in Human Judgement.*[4] According to the book, bias is when there is a systematic move or choice towards a particular direction, whereas noise is random differences in cases where the decisions should be the same. Taking the dart board analogy, if your darts are always to the left of the bullseye, you have a bias towards that direction, but if it is inconsistent all around the bullseye, that is noise. Noise could be created by various other factors—the current mood of the people, weather, group-think, etc. and it is random. The way to reduce both bias and noise is to use more objective data, more algorithms to aid decision-making and focus on delaying intuition through various mechanisms.

Before we design new processes, we need to identify and articulate the key elements of the company's culture that need to be reinforced. We will learn more about this in the coming chapters, but having a set of well-articulated core values helps set up the foundational processes.

Re-engineer all your systems and processes. Once you have identified the hotspots, based on the voice of employees, your own audit of key employee touchpoints, the legal imperatives and cultural values you want to reinforce, the key is to manage this in an integrated way. There are four key elements here:

1. **Set the tone at the top:** Make this important for the leadership. Your intent and commitment should come through clearly. As leaders, talk about your intent. Review complaints cases every quarter. Make yourself accessible and listen to any voice of frustration that may come to you. Get the team to publish regular data on this. Meet with the various 'employee experience' champion groups to hear them and show commitment. Hold managers accountable. Most organizations would already have a code of conduct, which is a must-have. But the best organizations translate this code of conduct into clear expected behaviours and communicate them. People copy others, especially those in positions of authority, when they are not very clear about the code of conduct. That's why the right role modelling by leaders has such a big impact.
2. **Re-architect systems and processes:** Our people systems can be classified into two broad areas—the systems and processes that could create a perception of unfairness, and those systems that take care of issues or complaints. Once you know the hotspots, fixing them could involve either complete re-engineering of that process or where it is not possible, putting in various nudges or control and review mechanisms. The use of data and analytics, at the point of decision-making, will help ensure fair decisions. For the systems that address issues or complaints, it is important to make them visible, independent and human, without employees fearing retaliation. Three questions to

ask here are: are these systems accessible to employees? Do employees trust them? Are they independent and command respect from all?

In my discussion with various Amazon teams, I found that they use an interesting concept called 'bias interrupter'. A scenario where this can be used is during a talent discussion about your team. Get a person who has no knowledge of your team to join your meeting just to ensure you follow the right process and to ask questions that make you reflect on possible biases. Moreover, in any recommendation for promotion, Amazon has a practice where the manager has to also fill up 'best reasons not to do this'. I think that is a good way to get diverse views and check biases. These kinds of processes ensure fairness.

3. **Educate and train managers:** As we saw earlier, managers have a key role to play in ensuring fairness. They are at the heart of creating an inclusive, psychologically safe workplace. While training them is critical, we need to reinforce the right culture by recognizing the right inclusive behaviour.
4. **Set up a robust feedback mechanism:** We need to track progress regularly and get feedback on how the systems are working. The team that tracks feedback should be different from the team that runs the people processes. Institutionalize the process for getting feedback—pulse surveys, regular focus groups, employee committees like the employee experience champions, etc. In Infosys, there is a Voice of Youth forum in each of the Development Centres (DC)—they participate in driving some of the employee activities in the DC, and also give feedback on any issues. Similarly, I was impressed

with this practice from Amazon India which has introduced a Voice of the Associate Board. People can write on the many whiteboards that have been placed across the floors of their offices about any issues they face—from lack of availability of packaging material to any grievance that they may have. The HR teams review this every day, and keep a record of all issues and resolutions. Such a visible redressal system sends a powerful message to the employees.

If this is done well, it would reflect in the voice of the employees—in engagement surveys, employee focus groups, etc. The number of complaints of wrong or unfair practices or behaviour can also decrease as a result. You will see a greater commitment to the team, and increase in psychological safety in the teams. Managers will demonstrate more inclusive behaviour and the overall culture of the company will also become more inclusive. It would be advisable to start tracking this by checking with various identity-groups on how inclusive and fair they perceive the organization or their team to be.

◆

Gangapriya Chakraverti, India Site Head and Managing Director, Ford Business Solutions:

What's the image that comes to your mind when you hear Ford? Cars obviously. But somewhere the idea of a **family** may also come along.

At Ford, the idea of every employee being part of the 'family' is foundational to the idea of fairness and inclusion. Employees are expected to care for each other through valuing diversity, embracing inclusion, celebrating success, encouraging new thinking, supporting each other through change and winning as a team. Supported by our code of conduct, equal opportunity employment guidelines, open door policy and zero tolerance for harassment doctrine, along with the emphasis on caring for each other, we bring to life our commitment to fairness and inclusion. I want to highlight four principles that aid us in keeping the family spirit alive.

1. **Defining boundaries:** Every family has its own set of values and code of conduct, mostly unwritten, but role modelled by elders. At Ford, the code of conduct is a sacrosanct document. And, as part of onboarding and orientation to the company, the details of the code are shared with new employees. Employees are periodically reminded of the code and any deviations from it are addressed appropriately.
2. **Maintaining transparency and confidentiality:** The onus of maintaining confidentiality of proprietary and sensitive information vests in the hands of the employees at Ford while leaders ensure a high level of transparency within the organization. Much gets shared with employees on a need to know basis—product updates, business plans, etc.—in the belief that they would guard sensitive information with care, like 'family secrets'. Employees are always informed about key organizational and personnel changes before they are shared to the wider public or

media. This, in turn, helps build trust in the organization which is essential for its success and sustenance.

3. **Valuing diversity:** Like in a family, each employee at Ford is considered unique, bringing unique capabilities to the organization and adding value to the company in their special way. Recognizing and embracing diversity is a fundamental value at Ford and differences are respected and celebrated.
4. **Ensuring psychological safety:** Families offer a sense of belonging, allowing their members to be their authentic selves in a psychologically safe environment. Family members also look out for each other's well-being. Ford, as an organization, strives to provide the same environment for its employees—with a focus on holistic well-being.

The rallying cry at Ford revolves around three ideas—'**We are family. We celebrate our differences. We belong.**'

◆

Design thinking is an approach to development or problem-solving by thinking like a designer. This approach brings together what is desirable from a human point of view with what is technologically feasible and economically viable. Desirability, feasibility and viability are three core pillars of thinking. Excellent resources are available at IDEO and the Stanford D School if you want to learn more about good design.[5] In summary, it is based on the principles of user centricity and empathy, collaboration, using a hands-on approach by testing prototypes, and is iterative.[6] It basically involves the following steps:

1. Empathize
2. Define
3. Ideate
4. Prototype
5. Test

Key Takeaways

- The foundation of any organization is fair and inclusive practices. That enables people to aspire to grow and be at their best. It is also the first step in ensuring psychological safety in teams. And finally, it is the right thing to do—as a humanitarian value as well as a principle of natural justice.
- The inclusion roadmap is a three-step process. First, ensure that you are complying with all regulations. Next, look at what your people expect and take care of those. But, the final one is a question you have to ask yourself: '*Will this make us what we want to be?*' What is the unique culture we want to build?
- When we look at fairness in organizations, we need to keep a focus on these three elements: Distributive justice (that right outcomes/decisions are delivered), procedural justice (that the process is seen as fair and consistent) and finally interactional justice (that the dignity of the individual is always upheld through all interactions).
- So how do we do it? A recommendation is to use the

principles of design thinking and understand what people experience and what they would like. Set up forums to understand views of various identify-groups. Do an audit of key employee touchpoints or moments of truth and find out which of these are not inclusive or fair. Also lay out your vision of what is the culture you would like to build in your organization.

- Finally, there are four key steps that we can take to make the difference. Start with the tone at the top—leadership role modelling is critical. Follow that up with rebuilding systems and processes and, where necessary, using data and analytics, to remove bias and bring in a fair process. Training and sensitizing managers is at the heart of this. Eventually, they are the ones who take decisions and run processes. Follow this up with transparent measurement and reporting.

References

1. J. Greenberg, 'A Taxonomy of Organizational Justice Theories,' *Academy of Management Review,* Vol. 12, 9–22, 1987.
2. Z. S. Bryne and R. Cropanzano, 'Fairness Reduces the Negative Effects of Organizational Politics on Turnover Intentions, Citizenship Behavior and Job Performance,' *Journal of Business and Psychology*, 2005, https://doi.org/10.1007/s10869-005-8258-0. Accessed on 4 September 2021.
   Also presented at the annual conference of the Society of Industrial and Organizational Psychology in New Orleans, Louisiana, 2000.

3. J.S. Adams, 'Inequality in Social Exchange', In L. Berkowitz (ed.), *Advances in Experimental Social Psychology*, Academic Press, 1965.
4. Daniel Kahneman, Cass R. Sunstein and Olivier Sibony, *Noise: A Flaw in Human Judgement*, William Collins, 2021.
5. 'Ideo', https://designthinking.ideo.com/. Accessed on 4 September 2021.
6. 'Stanford D School', https://dschool.stanford.edu/. Accessed on 4 September 2021.

5

A Hard Day's Night

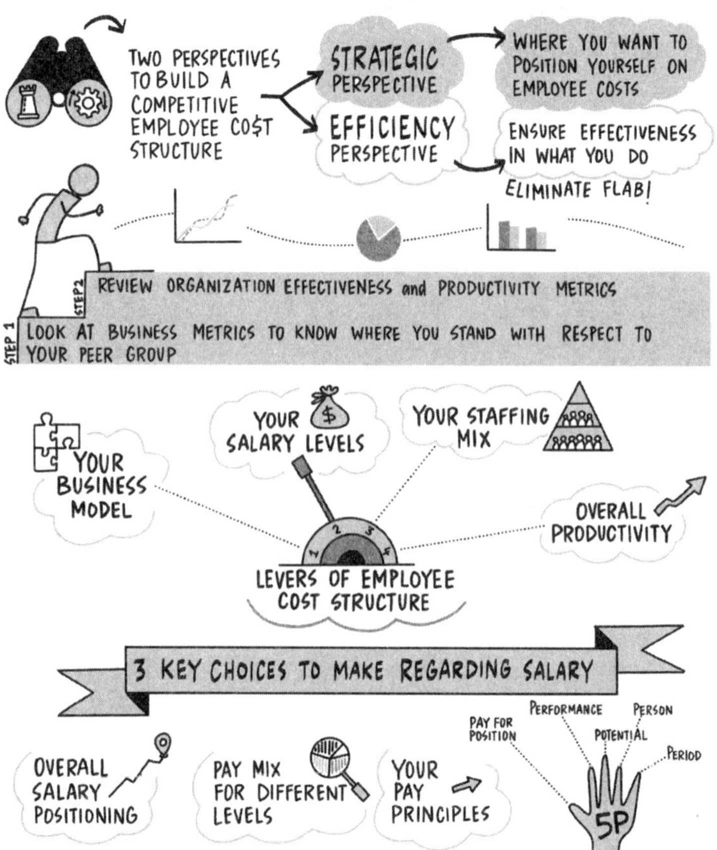
BUILDING COMPETITIVE COST STRUCTURES
TWO PERSPECTIVES TO BUILD A COMPETITIVE EMPLOYEE CO$T STRUCTURE
STRATEGIC PERSPECTIVE
WHERE YOU WANT TO POSITION YOURSELF ON EMPLOYEE COSTS
EFFICIENCY PERSPECTIVE
ENSURE EFFECTIVENESS IN WHAT YOU DO
ELIMINATE FLAB!
STEP 2 REVIEW ORGANIZATION EFFECTIVENESS and PRODUCTIVITY METRICS
STEP 1 LOOK AT BUSINESS METRICS TO KNOW WHERE YOU STAND WITH RESPECT TO YOUR PEER GROUP
YOUR SALARY LEVELS
YOUR STAFFING MIX
YOUR BUSINESS MODEL
OVERALL PRODUCTIVITY
1 2 3 4
LEVERS OF EMPLOYEE COST STRUCTURE
3 KEY CHOICES TO MAKE REGARDING SALARY
OVERALL SALARY POSITIONING
PAY MIX FOR DIFFERENT LEVELS
YOUR PAY PRINCIPLES
PAY FOR POSITION
PERFORMANCE
POTENTIAL
PERSON
PERIOD
5P

I have worked with many business leaders and have learnt a lot from them. I worked closely with the head of the beverages business at Unilever India, who had a reputation of 'cleaning up' businesses. There were a number of things I picked up from him while he went about transforming the beverages business. But one message stayed with me: 'You have to earn the right to grow.' What did that mean? Simply that you cannot invest for growth in a business if you are inefficient.

Getting to the right and efficient organization is critical for growth. As a start-up, you probably over-invest in capabilities to grow the business once you are sure that you have a viable proposition. But after the first few years, it is important to get to an efficient organization so you can be competitive. Are the people costs aligned to your value creation opportunities? Apart from the efficiency angle, there is this issue of a strategic choice. Of course, this is one of the strategic choices you could make. For instance, you could compete on being lowest cost in your industry, or on offering differentiated products or services. This strategy has to be designed into the organization you build.

One of the key outcomes that is needed in any business is to have a competitive people cost structure. Based on your strategy, you could decide where you could play—as a cost warrior or a differentiated player. In either case, you would probably need to know the different levers from a people perspective.

How important is employee cost to you? You may say this is not important. You might think, 'People cost is just 4 per cent of my revenue, so why should I spend time on it?' Fair point, but before you ignore this, I would urge you to consider two perspectives. First, look at how manageable your other costs are and the sensitivity of your margin to your employee costs. A 20 per cent gross margin business will need five times incremental revenue to pay for any incremental people cost, and that is just to maintain status quo profits. Second, it may be more than costs—it is also about productivity and agility. Even if you get a small improvement here, you could generate significant value for your business. Lastly, and very importantly, you need to look at where these people costs are disproportionately higher—are these in areas that are vital to your business or in other areas?

Take the fast-moving consumer goods (FMCG) industries. People costs here are normally at around 4–5 per cent of revenue, but the focus on efficiency, productivity and the challenge of improving margins puts a crucial focus on people organization and costs. You may be in a business where people costs are over 60 per cent of the revenue, like in professional services or IT services. Being cost-effective and productive is a great source of competitive advantage in these industries. But you don't take these calls in isolation—you look at people cost in terms of the talent availability, the business model and how important is talent attraction to you, and decide an optimal positioning considering all issues. In these businesses, people cost is a key lever and is the organization's focus. Hospitality is another industry where people costs are about 30 per cent of the revenue. Hence, people decisions are critical to the business model.

Therefore, there are two key vectors of looking at people costs: the strategic angle and the efficiency/focus angle. The key questions to answer would be:

1. What should be my strategic positioning on people costs?
2. Are the people costs aligned to my value creation opportunities?
3. What are the opportunities for improving efficiencies and effectiveness?

Let's dive into the levers of employee cost. Broadly, there are four key areas, and you could make significant strategic choices in each:

1. **Your business model:** that part of the value chain you are engaged in—you may choose to outsource some of your operations or have partners support you.
2. **Salary level:** your salary and benefits positioning.
3. **Staffing:** your overall workforce, your staffing by levels, the type of talent that you hire and onboard—the geographical spread of your talent
4. **Productivity:** how effective is your organization and what amplifies your productivity?

We will go through each of these levers and discuss the choices we can make. But before you do that, we need to dive into some numbers—something that will help us understand the full picture. I recommend that you do this analysis for your industry peer group.

Start with evaluating business-level metrics against your strategic positioning. It helps give you an overview of where you stand. You could follow that up by reviewing the organization effectiveness metrics and then the operational productivity metrics to get a view of potential hotspots.

Table 1
Key Productivity Metrics

<table>
<tr><th></th><th>The measure</th><th>How does it help</th></tr>
<tr><td colspan="3">Business level metrics</td></tr>
<tr><td>People cost efficiency</td><td>Employee cost as a % revenue</td><td rowspan="4">These measures give you a picture of your people cost, but need to be seen in the context of your strategy and business model.</td></tr>
<tr><td>Affordability ratio</td><td>Employee cost as a % earnings before interest and taxes (EBIT)</td></tr>
<tr><td>Overall value created per employee</td><td>Revenue/employee or Profit/employee</td></tr>
<tr><td>Human capital value added per employee</td><td>Total revenue less non-people costs/ employee</td></tr>
<tr><td colspan="3">Organization effectiveness metrics</td></tr>
<tr><td>Average span of control</td><td>For all managers, first-level managers and the top 50 or 100 leaders</td><td>Helps track management inefficiencies, especially in operating areas.</td></tr>
<tr><td>Organization depth</td><td>Number of reporting layers from frontlines sales to CEO (or shop floor operator to CEO)</td><td>You could set some guidelines for the operating functions and the others and check where you are. Ideally, five levels are recommended.</td></tr>
</table>

Teeth to tail ratio	Total sales and delivery headcount to rest of the functions	This helps keep the focus on revenue generating headcount
Leadership intensity	People in leadership level to total employees	You could define the level of leadership that is relevant to you. It helps in keeping a check on 'grade creep' and having a top heavy organization
Operational productivity metrics		
These would vary from industry to industry and you could choose a few critical ones: revenue/sales person, revenue/store, time measures, quality measures		

People Cost and Productivity Metrics

These are indicative metrics and all of them may not apply to your industry. For instance, the organization effectiveness metrics are suited to large organizations in manufacturing or IT services and may not work for all industries, especially start-ups. But identifying something similar makes sense and crafting some principles around it helps keeps the focus.

While you may get industry benchmarks for the business-level metrics, it may not be so easy for the others. Take the hospitality industry, for instance. Typically the industry follows a room to people ratio of 1:1.7. I would recommend that you treat this as a journey. Build your own path to improve these if you like. One good idea is to compare different business units within your organization to know what needs to be worked on.

Once you have analysed this against your strategic positioning, we could review each of the levers of being cost competitive.

Business Model

Clearly, there are certain choices of business models that you could make, deciding which part of the value chain you want to be fully engaged in and where you could be looking to partner with others. The supply chain is one area which can offer opportunities to partner with others to leverage scale and expertise, and also to enable you to focus on your core differentiating capabilities. Similarly, technology and routine business operations are areas for engaging with the larger eco-system. From the people perspective, three key factors play out for your decision-making in this regard—the people cost leverage, availability of career opportunities in those areas and reducing the complexity of people management.

The salary levels are a choice you make. Most organizations would aim to be at the median of the salary for each level. This means that your internal median salary would be similar to the industry median salary. If you want to attract top talent and be seen as a performance-oriented company, you could aim to be at the seventieth percentile for your high performers. If you want to play on costs, you may say that you would aim to have your internal median just below the industry median, with fresh entrants to that level join in at the tenth or the twentieth percentile. Setting these guidelines normally helps shape your compensation strategy.

The salary, or what people now call total rewards, generally consists three parts—a fixed pay, a variable pay or bonus (compensation experts call it 'short-term incentives') that is normally paid in the year and a long-term incentive (LTI) which is usually in the form of stock awards or incentive units. With increasing seniority, the 'pay at risk', which is the annual variable pay and the long-term incentives, will increase as part of the total rewards. This split of fixed, variable and long-term incentives is called the 'pay mix' in our rewards jargon. For firms which may be performance driven, another way of positioning is to be at the median of the industry for fixed pay, but at seventieth percentile for total compensation, which means a higher portion of pay at risk.

We normally start with paying for the position, but there could be pay for other things as well. For instance, you would pay for performance. The variable part of the total pay is fully dependent on performance. Even annual increases (increments) in fixed pay could be based on performance. Second, you could pay for potential. Unilever used to pay its high potential managers a premium of 10–15 per cent over the rest. The annual increments for high potential or a sustained high performer could even be double of what the others got. You could pay for the person—if someone brings unique skills and expertise, you could pay them a premium. As certain skills become scarce in the market, you would have to pay for these skills. In the technology industry, where the half-life of skills is short, certain key skills would command a premium.

Finally, pay could be linked to 'period'. Some kind of retention-based pay which is payable if a person completes a particular time on the rolls, used mainly for frontline staff in business process outsourcing (BPO) or retail, where employee turnover tends to be high. To summarize, we can pay for the position, performance, potential, person (skills) and period, or a mix of these. You could decide on a mix of these principles, given your industry-specific context, your strategy, positioning and talent availability.

So, the three key concepts that we can use to plan your salary costs are:

1. Your overall salary positioning based on your strategy
2. Your pay mix for different levels
3. Your pay principles—work creatively with the 5Ps (pay for position, performance, potential, person and period) to ensure that your needs are met

Staffing

While pay is determined by the market, creative staffing options can lead to significant competitive advantages and have an impact on your cost structure. But as we saw before, all these have to be considered in a holistic way, in line with your strategy, as each involves making some strategic choices. Here are some choices that you can make based on your industry and your specific strategic positioning:

1. **Internal vs external:** It's a choice you have to make in fast-growing industries where your employee turnover is reasonably high. Having a strong internal pipeline means you hire graduates from the campus, train them and get them ready for your roles. The advantage is that you have specifically trained staff. They will be short of

experience though, and thus it might take some time for them to be fully productive.

2. **Alternate talent source:** Investment in an alternate talent source could pay off in the long term but that would mean building that capability. For instance, when the rest of the industry is hiring engineers, you could choose to hire apprentices after school and support them with an engineering degree over five years as they work with you. The banking industry in India set up a school of banking to train graduates for a career in banking and ensure a steady pool of trained talent at low cost. Innovation is always possible and is the source of competitive advantage. With new skills getting scarce, building gig programmes will enable you to get the right talent. This helps create what they call the 'liquid workforce', enabling you to get talent on demand. 'Learn as you earn' programmes, leveraging the gig ecosystem and going to a different talent market are all ways to make your talent supply robust and competitive.
3. **The 'pyramid' choice:** Large IT services companies or manpower-intensive industries adopt a pyramid approach—large numbers of individual contributors at the entry level that fall off sharply as you look at managerial numbers. Setting guidelines for roles to be classified at each level helps in managing 'grade creep'—people doing the same job but moving up the organization hierarchy. Clear and transparent classification of roles and levels is beneficial to organizations.
4. **Skills partnerships:** In the age of fast-changing skills, set up partnerships for specific skills with organizations

that can either do the work for you or provide talent or train for you—there are partnerships at all levels and this will help you with building agility in your staffing process.

Staffing is a strategic choice—both the quantity and the profile of people you want at different levels—and this is a very big lever to build your competitive advantage.

Productivity

Finally, your organization's focus on productivity is a key determinant of your competitive cost structure. As with any discipline, this needs to be a tone that the top leadership sets. Clarifying the principles of how the organization will be designed and built is key to ensure sustained focus. This is more than just cost management. It builds agility and accountability in the organization, and hence, is truly part of the culture of the organization.

Let's go back to Table 1 on Key Productivity Metrics and look at the organization effectiveness metrics first. Organizations have a tendency to build some flab due to many priorities, initiative overload and the need to accommodate the personal growth of people and business continuity. The first step is to link these to the growth of the organization so that you are not increasing headcount out of line with your affordability. You can then zoom into the organization effectiveness metrics. While the guidelines may not work across the board in today's complex environment, you could choose certain key focus areas that may be relevant to your organization. For instance, for a large operating and sales organization, focusing on the right span of control and layers in the organization would make a lot of sense. If you are worried about a growing corporate office or a mushrooming leadership layer, look at the teeth to tail ratio or the leadership intensity ratios. I know of a big Indian conglomerate that looks at three key metrics as part of its people productivity assessment and business planning exercise: Employee cost as a percentage of revenue, employee cost as a percentage of gross margin and revenue per employee. Keeping this focus helps in driving productivity. Sometimes, it is not the cost that matters here but the potential inefficiency one additional person or layer can cause.

Even shop floors have become delayered. Teams that can multitask and are self-managed can pave the way for a more empowered organization.

As we look at the post-pandemic future for organization design, it is clear that we may rethink some of our existing assumptions. What kind of work can be done remotely in lower cost locations? Do we need several layers to manage work? Maybe the span of control could change, given the rapid increase in digitization. It is time to rethink our organization.

The next phase is to delve into operational productivity areas. The focus here could be to see how we could improve a few areas with an integrated approach to process, technology, training and the right talent. Companies that make operational excellence a part of their DNA prioritize areas for improvement, track them regularly, put cross-functional teams to work on them and improve them.

Manoj Kohli, who, in his role as Country Head, SoftBank, mentors over 25 start-ups that are disrupting diverse industries using technology, explains what is critical for start-ups as they try and scale up.

In my many interactions with start-ups, I find that the scaling-up challenge is the one they find the toughest. Growth without margin is dangerous; we should aim for profitable growth. Unsustainable growth means you will have to restructure, which is a loss of reputation. And that's why productivity is crucial for them.

The question I like to ask them is, 'How do you make sure that you don't have one extra person anywhere?' This is what I would normally recommend to them. Make your growth plan for the next 36 months. By every quarter, estimate the growth of customers, revenue, manpower, manpower cost and productivity. Are you getting economies of scale? Are you driving end-to-end digitization?

Closely watching the productivity metrics will help to avoid any false steps. This puts the focus on the intrinsic performance of the business, making it sustainable.

Start-ups, in my mind, have many challenges—developing a unique and profitable business model, building their brand, engaging a strong leadership team, maintaining high performance, work ethic and compliance and ethics. The problems in a start-up become visible when it is starting to scale-up. Therefore, productivity focus, building a culture and a hungry attitude are important.

If people productivity goes wrong, it can lead to reputation loss when you try and correct it. Moreover, it hurts the morale of other employees. Therefore, it is prudent to focus on it rigorously from the beginning.

Key Takeaways

- You build a competitive employee cost structure by looking at two vectors—the strategic perspective and the efficiency perspective.
- The strategic perspective is about where you want to be positioning yourself in terms of employee cost, while the efficiency perspective is to ensure that you are effective in what you set out to do.
- The first step is to look at a set of business-level metrics to understand where you stand with respect to your peer group, and then follow it up by reviewing organization effectiveness metrics and the operational productivity ones.
- There are four key levers when you look at your employee cost structure—your business model, your salary levels, your staffing mix and overall productivity.
- There are three key choices to make regarding salary—your overall salary positioning based on your strategy, your pay mix for different levels and finally your pay principles—the 5Ps (pay for position, performance, potential, person and period) to ensure that your needs are met.
- Your staffing choices could be based on the type of talent sources you can tap into. There have been various innovations in this area, including gig work and staffing partnerships.
- Lastly, you drive productivity in the organization and build a culture through a rigorous monitoring of key productivity metrics.

6

New Kid in Town

FINDING RIGHT TALENT

EFFECTIVENESS OF A PERSON IN A JOB = f(TALENT × JOB DESIGN × TEAM CLIMATE)

THERE IS NO UNIVERSAL 'RIGHT TALENT'! DEPENDS ON YOUR CONTEXT

BRAND ESSENCE
THE SINGLE DIFFERENTIATING FACTOR

BRAND PERSONALITY
IF COMPANY WERE A PERSON, HOW WOULD THEY BE?

EMOTIONAL BENEFITS
HOW DOES COMPANY MAKE YOU FEEL?

FUNCTIONAL BENEFITS
EMPLOYER VALUE PROPOSITION

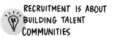

RECRUITMENT IS ABOUT BUILDING TALENT COMMUNITIES

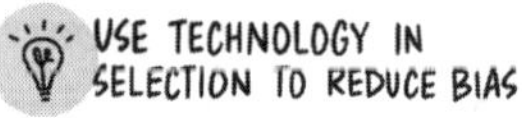

About two decades ago, McKinsey published the paper 'War for Talent'.[1] Over the years, that war has become part of everyday business. Attracting and retaining the right talent is now 'par for the course'—it has become a bare necessity! Think about the biggest breakthroughs or successes you have had in your business, compared to the competition. What went into it? Of course there will be a leadership vision, some outstanding teamwork, but there will always be the right people in the right jobs at that time. Needless to say, the right talent is the key to success, especially as you look to break away and lead your competitive pack. That is at the heart of our third foundational outcome: attracting and engaging the right talent, and ensuring you have the right talent for the right jobs at the right time!

Consider a person doing a job. What factors go into making her or him effective? Skills, mindset, behaviours (let's call all of this 'talent') and also the job (the design, its empowerment) as well as the climate of the team the person is working in. Let's try and express this as:

Effectiveness of a person in a job = f (Talent x Job Design x Team Climate)

While this equation holds true, the weightage of each of the three factors depends upon the type of role and organization. For routine operational roles, all three elements of the above equation would be equally important but for innovation-oriented roles or leadership roles, the weightage on the quality of talent would be much higher. For instance, in a start-up, this quality of talent can be crucial because it can shape the job and the team climate. Therefore, the quality of talent can make a proportionately bigger difference, especially in more dynamic, less structured environments.

Here, we have a caveat. Talent means something specific for that role and organization—having the specific skills and behaviours that are appropriate in that role and organization. Thus, talent has a context in which it flourishes. Boris Groysberg, professor of business administration at Harvard Business School, talks of five key elements that are relevant for success. The leadership competencies of the individual, the skills or functional expertise needed for that role, the internal connections, the external connections and the experience of similar situations before.[2] Some jobs may need a high element of internal connections, and an external person may experience difficulties in doing it.

So how do we attract the right talent? But before that, do we know what is the right talent for your organization and for each job? Let's start with that.

What Is Right Talent?

It is important that you define what the right talent is for you at two levels—first, at the strategic level and then at the more functional level. What do I mean by that? Let me explain.

Let's go back to the earlier chapter on thinking about your strategy. If you have a differentiated strategy, what kind of behaviours are essential for the success of that strategy? What is it that you would like all your people to demonstrate? Perhaps, we can discuss some examples, and maybe begin with the much quoted Southwest Airlines. The Airlines believes in fun and keeping customers happy, so it is clearly the one thing it will look for in its people—the ability to be cheerful and to cheer up customers. Similarly, a company like Disney will look for the ability to connect with people. A company that thrives on innovation will look for people with curiosity and the ability to collaborate. Execution-focused companies will look for a bias for action. Technology companies may look for the ability to learn new concepts easily to keep up with the fast-changing skill-set requirements of the tech industry. Again, this is based on your strategy—if it is truly differentiated, you would need people with the relevant mindset and behaviours to make it successful. The behaviours you look for in talent could also connect to your purpose as a company or your values, but try and distil one or two key elements of mindset or behaviour that are critical for your success.

The next step is quite easy. There are four key elements that make up the right talent, what I call the **SBEM** framework:

1. The functional **skills** needed for the job
2. The **behaviours** that are necessary for success (what we HR folk call 'competencies')
3. The right **experiences** people need to have had
4. The **mindset**—their attitude and the purpose that drives them

The first two are quite simple—to know what to do and how to do the job. Also, keep in mind that the requirements for a job are closely linked to the challenges and priorities at that time. Moreover, the skills and behaviours of the right talent should match that job context.

Finding talent with the right experiences can be tricky. The right job experiences teach you a lot more than just the skills. Experiences introduce individuals to the contexts, people and challenges that mould them. When you look to hire people in leadership roles, the right job experiences become more valuable, as they give you better insight into the person's capabilities. The medals and scars that people acquire from their experiences are great teachers.

However, one can argue that in these times of rapid change, what you may have done in the past may not be relevant. In a way, it is a fair challenge. But this experience gives you some critical boost in key jobs. For instance, if you have turned around a failing business or grown a business, you are more likely to have the skills and mindset required to succeed in a start-up, as opposed to someone who has been in mature, low-growth businesses.

Finally, comes the mindset or attitude. This is more about what drives them, and what their philosophy of life and success is. Do they have a learning mindset? Do they think more about themselves or about the larger cause? What do they value? In most cases, you will look for the attitude that is aligned to your strategic need. It is important to note that this is not a laundry list. They need to be just one or two well-considered and clearly differentiated mindset areas.

So, as you can see, there is no talent that would be universally suited. The talent should be suited to the context, both for the organization and for the job at the time. Oftentimes, thinking about the right talent entails thinking about talent differently by looking for skill-sets that compliment the organization. Therefore, rather than looking for the answer to the question 'Who is the right talent?', it may be better to ask:

1. What are the different strategic priorities for this business?

2. Does my team have all the skills to address this?
3. Do I need to recruit with a different lens?

Now that you have defined what the right talent for you is, how do you go about attracting that talent in an institutionalized way? You could attract a few with your personal focus but how would you make this intrinsic to your business's functioning? My suggestion would be to, first, think of your 'employer brand'.

The employer brand refers to the company's identity as an employer. The employer brand of a company will exist regardless of the company's conscious decision to develop it. Whereas, employer branding refers to the discipline of defining, developing and managing a company's brand or reputation as an employer. Branding applies the proven principles of brand management to employee experience in order to be capable of recruiting top talent.[3] For instance, let's look at the Tata employer brand. It is strongly associated with trust, ethics and reliability. This perception is based on the way the organization is seen as a 'place to work' by potential recruits, current employees, leavers and retirees. But can you consciously build and manage it? That is the key.

We are in the digital world of information, perception, opinions and social media—all in a competitive talent market. How do you stand out from the crowd as an employer? Here is an example that many of us may be familiar with. Google says, 'Do cool things that matter'[4] and that gets manifested in their brand attributes and pervades their culture. Glassdoor, LinkedIn and many others have created a very open and transparent platform that candidates use to decide on their potential employers. According to research conducted by Glassdoor, 75 per cent of active job seekers are likely to apply to a job if the employer actively manages their employer brand.[5]

So how do we build an employer brand? While you will find a lot of tactical actions on the internet and in various employer brand kits, the key is to go back to the principles of a brand. Define the essence of your employer brand. This should come from your core strategy, your corporate brand and the culture you have in the organization or the one you aspire towards. What is at the heart of your employee experience?

Anuradha Razdan, CHRO, Hindustan Unilever, who led the development of the new employer brand for Unilever has this tip:

> Ask what is unique to your brand that no one else can replicate—the answer to this would lie in the strengths and traits that make your organization unique. And this is as much defined by those inside the organization as by those on the outside who find your organization aspirational. Often those within the organization don't appreciate what is attractive to those aspiring to enter the organization.[6]

This is the single intangible attribute that differentiates your brand from others. The next step is to articulate your brand personality—what would the personality of your employer brand be if it were an individual? How would they behave and talk? These are human traits associated with the brand. This is the way the brand communicates with its users, employees and potential recruits.

Further, articulate the emotional and functional benefits of the employer brand. Emotional benefits refer to how the company as an employer makes an employee feel.

Functional benefits refer to the Employer Value Proposition (EVP), the unique set of benefits a company offers to its employees in exchange for their skill set. The EVP is what attracts fresh talent and helps retain existing talent. The EVP is what will make your employer brand come alive.

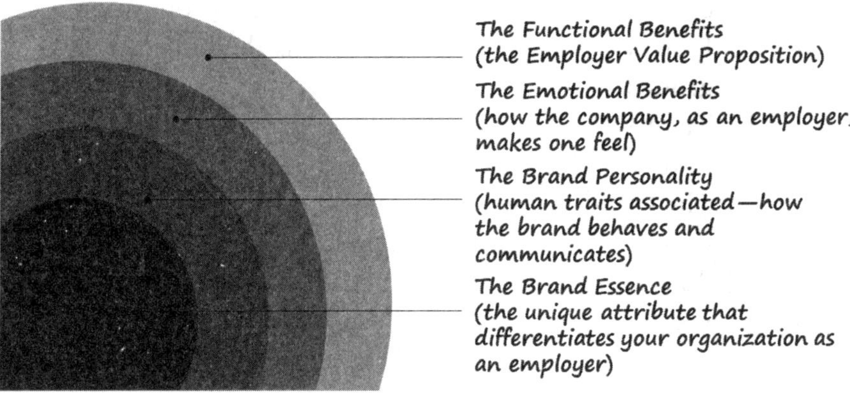

The EVP is the articulation of the employer brand, answering the questions, 'Why should I work for your company?' and 'Why should I stay in this company?' Employer brand is the reputation and EVP is the narrative. It's everything your company can offer as an employer in exchange for all the skills and experience your employees bring to the table. The value proposition describes what an organization stands for, requires and offers as an employer. The EVP needs to be derived from the brand essence and aligned to the brand essence. In a way, the EVP has to bring the employer brand alive.

From my experience, here are a couple of points about the EVP that we need to keep in mind:

1. Elements of the EVP could be different for different personas in the organization—the middle manager, the frontline salesforce and the workmen in the factory. For each of these personas, you could have a clearly articulated proposition. However, the core essence remains the same across groups.
2. The EVP needs to be refreshed regularly so that it is in tune with the needs and aspirations of employees. The brand essence is the same, but the expression in terms of features could change.
3. As you start building your EVP, the first step is to speak to your employees, especially the newer ones joining the workforce. What elements of the work and culture do they value more?
4. Once you get the pulse of the people, look at your own employer brand and your strengths and uniqueness as an employer. Build the new EVP from your brand essence.
5. I have seen that an effective EVP integrates and aligns the whole work experience, from culture, mission and values, to total rewards through jobs and people. Take all the elements that are important to an employee in a job/organization and articulate your proposition on that element, aligned to your employer brand. For instance, if your employer brand is all about 'the Power of You', you would craft the EVP along these lines:
    a. You can choose any career in the company without any functional barriers.

   b. You can leverage your strengths by applying for gig work within any part of the company.
   c. We will have a personalized and flexible rewards and benefits package for you.
   d. Our culture values diversity in all forms and we encourage diverse teams.
6. Having a clear employer brand and EVP also guides the actions of the managers and the HR teams. Communicate the EVP to both current and prospective employees.
7. Finally, do regular reviews and dipstick checks to see you are on track.

If you are able to build a differentiated employer brand, and consistently bring it to life through sustained actions supported by an EVP, you will attract the kind of people you want. Activating your employer brand and EVP is important. Borrowing from the work on consumer brands, we also need to have an 'activation strategy' to bring this to life through an integrated set of actions. Develop a 'signature' activity or event that stands out as an example of your employer brand. For instance, Adecco has a practice of having young people from across the globe become the 'CEO' for a month, shadowing the CEO.[7] Moreover, what I have seen as core to a great employer brand is consistent communication from leaders and employees. The key to this is consistency. When I spoke to Girish Menon, the CHRO of Swiggy, he said there were three key levers for the 'excitement hook' for their people—the culture, the learning and differentiated rewards and wealth creation opportunities. These are the core elements of their EVP.

Another good example of an employer brand and

EVP done right is Merck, the American multinational pharmaceutical company. Their employer brand tagline, 'Bring your curiosity to life' encourages a 'continuous cycle of invention, making an impact and using that to inspire internally and externally.'[8] At Merck, it's important to have a genuine connection with the work one does. The company takes the stance that not only do each of its 68,000 employees have a significant story, but also that each of those stories serve as an inspiration to do great work.[9]

The Employee Experience

In a fast-changing world where people have access to information, social media and a set of high expectations, there is an emerging school of thought that we need to go beyond the EVP and look at the employee experience at each touchpoint, as these experiences build the overall perception about the company. This involves mapping the key touchpoints in the lifecycle of an employee in the company and identifying the emotions experienced in each of these. It clearly outlines all the touchpoints where employees experience negative emotions, and you could review those and transform those moments for them. Some of these touchpoints are the moments of truth for your employer brand. As we move to more virtual working, this aspect of digital experience for employees across all touchpoints will be critical.

Once you have a well-constructed employer brand and a robust and well-articulated EVP, you have to plan its execution. Let your employees communicate what they think of the company as an employer; enable them and amplify their opinions. Think of your brand personality as you articulate your employer brand. Is your brand personality interesting, self-deprecating, no-nonsense? Communicate on the lines of your brand personality and, soon, you will build a strong, vibrant employer brand.

One phrase I dislike is Talent Acquisition (TA). Getting people to join you is all about enlisting them for a cause—mobilizing people to join in creating something big and memorable. This is a responsibility that every manager needs to undertake to attract people. It is a narrative of the possibility, the dream, of a successful career that you offer people.

Organizations that make hiring a TA process and hand the responsibility to a TA team may not have the people you really need. It should be the leaders at the forefront, inspiring people with their vision and onboarding the ones they feel will make a difference. The best companies I have seen are those where every manager takes the responsibility of being a talent magnet. The HR or recruitment team can help with owning the employer brand, setting up partnerships, communicating and building a talent community. The talent community is made up of every potential employee that fits your description of 'right talent'—either as a full-time employee, a gig worker or a partner.

Table 2
Attracting Talent Is Everyone's Role

Role of the HR team	Every manager's role
Own the employer brand and EVP	Be a role model
Build the talent community	Be a talent magnet
Build the ecosystem of talent pools	Engage the talent community

As we look into the future, the role of the recruitment team would be to build this talent community, this potential pipeline of candidates, gig-workers or service providers, ensuring diversity. Curating such a talent community and engaging with this diverse talent pool are key areas to focus on. Look for alternate pools of talent and build talent partnerships that can add to your competitive advantage.

Finally, in our endeavour to attract the right talent, we come to the final selection. If you have worked on the employer brand, the EVP and on communicating and engaging the talent community, you should have a great set of people to select from. Every selection interaction is also one in which the candidate is coming to a decision about you, the prospective employer. And every person you choose not to select would be a candidate sometime in the future.

Research shows that other than seeing how someone performs on the job, the next best way to ascertain a candidate's suitability is through a structured interview. When asked what Shell's stand-out applicants have in common, one of their recruitment managers cited their ability to provide strong examples that help in assessing their potential. At Shell, they call this CAR or Capacity, Achievement and Relationships. 'Capacity explores a candidate's potential to analyse a situation and consider solutions to address problems or develop opportunities. Achievement demonstrates what you have done to deliver a result and whether you are able to adapt and learn from your achievements. Relationships are how you collaborate and work well with others.'[10] Following the popular STAR model (Situation, Task, Action, Result) is another good way to understand specific behaviours.

Research tells us that many biases come into play when we select people, the biggest one being that we select people in our image. Second, we normally make up our minds in the first few minutes of an interaction and then look for confirmatory clues. And there is the halo effect. We mistake good communication for good capability and skill. Daniel Kahneman cites an example of the time he had introduced a scoring system for hiring recruits to the Israeli army. He identified a few attributes and asked the interviewers to score the candidates on each of the attributes. The total of their scores would identify the right candidates. But the interviewers protested and didn't want their personal judgement to be lost in the process. In a compromise, the interviewers agreed to score the candidates on the attributes Kahneman had provided them and finally take an overall judgement call. As it turned out, the mere fact of having to think and score on the basis of the attributes influenced how the interviewers finally judged a candidate. Therefore, his tip is that we should try and delay our intuition to enable better decision-making. Setting up processes that allow one to think and reflect objectively helps to reduce biases. That's why algorithms that come up with logically derived, data-based outcomes reduce human biases, even if the final decision is left to the manager.[11]

The key here is to reduce all biases. Therefore, to start off, it would be good to first acknowledge all biases possible. So here is what I think are some tips for good selection:

1. Remember, you are hiring for a role. Before you meet anyone, write down the key challenges in the role and the desirable skills, behaviours, experiences and mindset, the SBEM, needed for a successful person.

2. Focus on their experiences and the skills and behaviours they have demonstrated.
3. It would be advisable to take feedback from at least two people from diverse backgrounds to cut down on bias.
4. Selection is always a leap of faith. Take a chance on someone who can grow into the job and can learn.

But the best way to eliminate bias is through the use of technology. Most selection processes run through a minimum of three or four funnels before a final decision is made—an initial shortlist of CVs, a first round of preliminary screening and maybe a minimum of two rounds of interviews. At least three of these four funnels should be done using technology—bots, Virtual Reality and AI. Objective proctored tests, virtual role play, case studies, hackathons, etc. are all great ways to select people using technology. Clearly, tests that measure behaviour like 'what will you do in these situations' are ideal. After the various virtual rounds, maybe there could be one final round with people, but all others could be done using technology. These help scale up your processes and reduce bias, but as you can imagine, these have to be designed and thought through clearly. Take, for instance, the practices followed by Swiggy, when they recruit employees for their technology teams. They hire for competence and believe that exposure is greater than education. Therefore, they do not look for the pedigree of the recruit's education. Instead, they conduct a four-level interview that emphasises on actual hands-on coding exercises. Selection is based on problem-solving skills and quality of coding.

Regular validation checks of the process with specific focus on rooting out biases, with a strong focus on construct validity and predictive validity would be essential. I would recommend that we check for bias in three key areas:

1. Does it discriminate against any gender or ethnic group?
2. Does it discriminate against economic status, background or age?
3. How are the selected candidates performing? Is there a bias against performance?

This also throws up some new roles for the future; someone to coach the bots on how to read emotions in candidate responses and react accordingly. People with an understanding of technology and human behaviour will be needed to build good selection systems, along with experts who understand how to determine bias and weed it out.

I can see that the next decade will be game-changing when it comes to attracting and selecting talent—a big area for all of us to focus on.

Anuradha Razdan, CHRO, Hindustan Unilever, who worked on shaping the Unilever Employer Brand says:

Whilst shaping the Unilever Employer Brand, we asked ourselves the question: what is 'Uniquely Unilever' that makes talent want to join us over other career options? It is as important to ask our own employees the answer to this question as it is to ask external talent because often our strengths are best understood through the eyes of outsiders. Having defined a powerful employer brand, consistency is key. How can we ensure this? Communicate, simply but sharply, the real experiences of real leaders. The biggest amplifier to our employer brand today is the use of digital tools and social media. But, I really believe that it pays to stick to the essence of our brand by being boringly consistent and authentic. Like for any successful product brand, employer brand perception is formed through patterns that talent observe over a period of time.

Key Takeaways

- A person's effectiveness in a job is a function of the person's talent (skills, behaviours, mindset), the job design (empowerment, linkages) and the team climate.
- Each of us has to decide on what is the right talent for us. The right talent for a role depends on the context of the role and the company. To decide this, we need to link it to our differentiated strategy—what kind of people are needed in line with our strategy.
- Talent can be defined in terms of SBEM: skills, behaviours, experiences and mindset. There is no universal 'right talent'. It depends on your context.
- To attract the right talent, articulate your employer brand. This is a mental model of what you are as an employer. It consists of a brand essence (the core of the brand—what is that single differentiating factor?), a brand personality (if the company were a person, what would they be like?), some emotional benefits (how does the company make you feel?) and the functional benefits (EVP).

- The EVP is a statement of the employer brand. It's everything that a company can offer as an employer, in exchange for all the skills and experience its employees bring to the table. The EVP, if fully delivered, will make the employer brand come alive.
- Recruitment is, essentially, the creation and expansion of the community's talent community—a community of potential hires. Ideally, every manager must be a talent magnet for the organization. While the HR team can build the talent pools and communities, the manager's role must be to engage with the talent community.
- Selection can be improved by using technology in various simulations, tests and interviews. This reduces bias. However, these need to be thoughtfully designed so that they make an unbiased selection.

References

1. Ed Michaels, Helen Handfield-Jones and Beth Axelrod, *War for Talent*, Harvard Business Publishing, 2001.
2. Boris Groysberg, *Chasing Stars: the Myth of Talent and the Portability of Performance*, Princeton University Press, 2010.
3. 'Employer Branding 101: Why, How and Proven ROI', Glassdoor, https://www.glassdoor.com/employers/resources/employer-branding-101-why-how-and-proven-roi/#what-is-employer-branding. Accessed on 5 September 2021.
4. 'Students', Google for Education, https://edu.google.com/students/index.html. Accessed on 20 October 2021.
5. Sarah A. Lybrand, 'What is Employer Branding and How Can it Grow Your Business?' LinkedIn Talent Blog, 1 March 2018, https://business.linkedin.com/talent-solutions/blog/

employer-brand/2018/employer-branding. Accessed on 5 September 2021.

6. Jorgen Sundberg, 'How Unilever Developed a New EVP and Employer Brand,' LinkHumans, https://linkhumans.com/unilever. Accessed on 5 September 2021.
7. 'CEO for One Month', Adecco, https://www.adeccogroup.com/ceoforonemonth/. Accessed on 20 October 2021.
8. Jorgen Sundberg, 'How Merck Trusts Employees to Activate the Employer Brand', LinkHumans, https://linkhumans.com/merck-employer-brand/. Accessed on 5 September 2021.
9. 'Case Study: Employer Branding at Merck,' 17 June 2020, Randstad, https://www.randstad.com/workforce-insights/employer-branding/case-study-employer-branding-merck/. Accessed on 5 September 2021.
10. '4 Ways to Stand Out as a Candidate', Shell, https://www.shell.com/careers/candidate-resource-centre/four-ways-to-stand-out-as-a-candidate. Accessed on 5 September 2021.
11. Daniel Kahneman, *Thinking Fast and Slow*, Penguin, 2011.

7

ENSURING RIGHT EXECUTION

EFFECTIVE EXECUTION IS AT THE HEART OF EVERY SUCCESSFUL BUSINESS

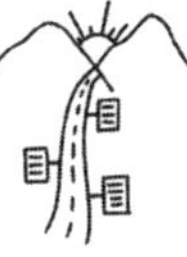

A. IDENTIFY KEY STRATEGIC INITIATIVES (focus on 3–4 key areas)

B. CLEARLY ARTICULATE AND COMMUNICATE THESE

STRATEGIC GOALS

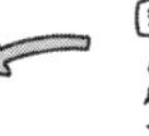

OPERATIONAL GOALS (sustain the momentum)

TRANSFORMATIONAL OBJECTIVES (shift the curve)

COMPANY or UNIT GOALS v/s INDIVIDUAL GOALS

FIXED v/s FLEXIBLE GOALS

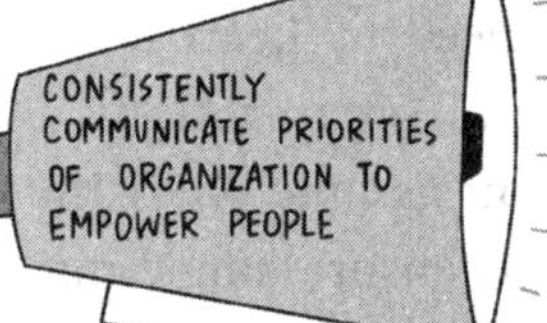

CONSISTENTLY COMMUNICATE PRIORITIES OF ORGANIZATION TO EMPOWER PEOPLE

FIND THE RIGHT BALANCE DEPENDING ON YOUR CONTEXT

THE FUTURE COULD BE MORE ABOUT **AGILE GOAL-SETTING PROCESSES,** WITH TEAM GOALS

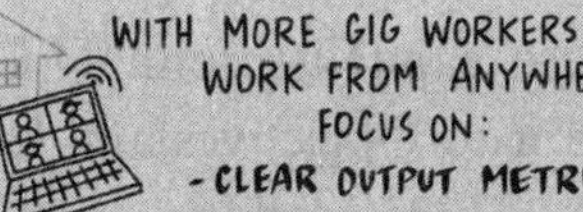

WITH MORE GIG WORKERS AND WORK FROM ANYWHERE, FOCUS ON:
- CLEAR OUTPUT METRICS
- GOOD FEEDBACK SYSTEM

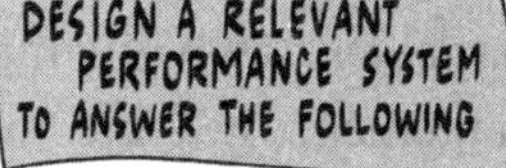

- Does the individual know how they performed and areas to focus on?
- Does the organization have a credible way to record individual's performance and link this to rewards in a fair way?
- Is the execution focus of the organization strengthened?
- Are people feeling energized for the future?

Execution! That's at the heart of this outcome: how can you get the results that you had planned for and expected from your strategy. Larry Bossidy and Ram Charan made this a mantra.[1] What use is a brilliant strategy if you cannot execute it? We all know of companies, with great ideas and strategy, that have faded away. Equally, we know of companies that have been successful with a single-minded focus on execution.

Many companies have found their secret sauce of execution. Over the years, each of them has built a strong process and cadence for execution. But what can we learn from all these ideas? For someone looking to set up a good process of getting strategy into action, what are some things we need to keep in mind? I have worked with leaders at several organizations and each had their unique style; but if you ask me what the one winning ingredient is, it would be to ensure single-minded focus!

But let's go back to the beginning. Some of the original ideas on this come from Peter Drucker's *The Practice of Management* which introduces the concept of MBO—Management by Objectives. As he writes, 'efficiency is doing things right; effectiveness is doing the right things.'[2] Setting objectives is about identifying the right things to do.[3]

Various schools of thought have followed this in getting strategy executed. Andrew Stephen Grove of Intel propounded a modified MBO framework, which became a hit with Silicon Valley once venture capitalist John Doerr brought it to Google and converted it to Objectives and Key Results, popularly known as OKRs.[4] There is another school of thought that focuses on communication and culture, with the belief that if the larger goals of the organization are shared openly that will help align people to get the strategy executed. A third school of thought believes that control systems and technology are the key to ensuring strategy execution.

Getting this engine right is the key to any organization's success. In my early years at Unilever, I underwent many a training programme, and then conducted a few as well, on how to write good objectives. We called them SMART objectives in those days—specific, measurable, achievable, relevant and time-bound objectives. Our business heads used to spend time crafting the objectives in the right way. It was quite a discipline and one of the reasons for HUL's success. And at the end of the year, we had to grade ourselves against each objective and state if we had fully achieved, partially achieved or not achieved those three objectives. If you had people with all three fully achieved, they would get back saying the objectives were not stretched enough!

Over the years, I have seen a lot of time spent by leaders on this process of goal setting, and I sometimes wondered whether it was worth all that effort. Employees would fret about their goals just because it will have an impact on their overall performance assessment. In one organization, everyone in sales had an identical set of operational goals, with the express reason that it would help compare people and their performance. But the contexts were different and the changes during the year made it difficult to make a simple comparison, and led to using some managerial judgement in deciding performance. So there are no easy answers here.

However, having been through this process for many years, I will try and outline the key questions that need to be answered and the choices we need to make.

1. Have we identified the key initiatives or focus areas that will help achieve our strategy? Are these clearly articulated and communicated? These are specific focus areas and it is recommended to have an overall number associated with each of them. You should ideally have between three to five such key areas. Some of these could be achieved in a year and while others could take a couple of years. If I were to think of a consumer goods firm, the following could be a set of key strategic focus areas:
    a. Gain shares in the personal care business
    b. Increase the sustainability footprint in our supply chain
    c. Make the organization 'fit for growth'
    d. Increase the share of wallet with key retail chains and grocery e-commerce

    In the past, companies have favoured the balanced scorecard. While it is still a good practice to ensure that you have a balanced scorecard at an enterprise- or a company-level, it would be a mistake to translate this into objectives for leaders. Objectives and goals should be linked to what you want to drive strategically.
2. What is our balance between sustaining current momentum and driving new initiatives that will change trajectory of the business? This is a philosophical question. From my experience, I see that strong execution-oriented, operationally-intensive companies focus more on sustaining the momentum, with standard goals that are consistent over time. However, companies that are focused on innovation or product-led growth, like FMCG

and technology product companies, would focus on goals linked to new initiatives, product launches, brand relaunches, etc. But personally, I would think that we need a mix of operational goals and transformational objectives for all leadership roles. In addition to the 'what' of the goals, there are two other things to look at—'how much' and 'how'? While the operational goals are straightforward and you only need to answer the 'how much' part by stating a target, the transformational goals would have a mix of both the 'how' and 'how much'. Let me give you an example.

An operational goal would be revenue growth at 10 per cent.

A transformational goal would be increasing your market share in personal care to 30 per cent by entering the natural herbal shampoo segment. Or this: focus on the post-paid segment through bundled products and grow at 20 per cent.

You see how these transformation goals also give a strategic direction, and that's why they help make the difference. If you go back to what Peter Drucker had in mind when he spoke of management by objectives, he had these kinds of transformational goals. Objectives intend to change the trajectory linked to your strategy.

Also, there are companies like 3M that allow people to take up innovative projects of their own for up to 15 per cent of the time. This was primarily an idea that started in their research teams. They have a practice where internal 'VCs' could assess the best ideas and agree funding.

3. The 'line of sight' debate—to what extent should we have overall company goals as part of an individual's overall goals? I have been through this debate a lot. One school of thought is that if people have their sights set on the overall company goals, they are focused on ensuring overall success of the company, and it increases collaboration and enterprise thinking. Equally, another group would say that people down the hierarchy don't have a 'line of sight' as to how their performance can impact the company goals. On the whole, getting people focused on the overall goals of the organization is good. However, at the lower levels, putting company goals as part of their set of objectives for the year may not work, while for senior levels this is absolutely necessary. You have to decide what makes sense in your organization; up to which level does it benefit to have specific goals clearly in your annual objectives. My recommendation would be that for the top two levels reporting to the CEO, some percentage of their goals should be clearly specified company goals. For the lower levels, the answer could be to link their overall bonus kitty to company performance. That way, they know if the company meets its targets, they may get a better variable pay.
4. Another choice we need to make is between a process of deep communication to enable people to decide goals by themselves versus a system of a cascading pre-set goal template. Basically it is the extent to which you want to control the kind of goals that people are setting. As technology pervades

this process, the advantage of having a standard set of goals is that you can get data on actual performance updated at regular intervals so people know where they are. Many HRM systems have also nudged us towards such standardization. That's the tyranny of these systems. Moreover, it helps getting everyone in the organization aligned to the key focus areas. It's a more like a 'factory approach'—it helps drive execution. I have seen companies that roll out a standard set of goals, with the thought that this will enable comparison among similar levels, create more objective performance data and help execution. Clearly, if you are an execution-focused company or in an industry where execution is key, like telecom or IT services, this could be a good method to adopt. The downside, of course, is that it reduces the scope for innovation and removes flexibility. Therefore, if you are in a business where you have disparate product groups and need differentiated focus, you have to give them more flexibility in line with the broad strategy; a standard template driven approach won't work.

One middle way is to create a library of goals that are quite varied and people can choose from them, while they still provide flexibility for them to add something unique. For example, Bhartiya Fashion, a leading fashion designer and manufacturer, has a unique repository of goals and objectives which is, by and large, common across unique roles in the company. The targets, of course, flow from the annual business plan for each category. These goals are available to the employees on the HR portal and are reviewed every year to align with that year's specific thrust area.

Goals and measures shape behaviour. Consider what P&G did in the early 2000s when it realized that it needed to foster greater innovation. The company did a major study to identify the leadership behaviours that were necessary to achieve that objective and implemented a new performance evaluation system that emphasized on various key attributes, including the ability to generate innovations by building collaborative relationships. Those criteria were then used to assess managers regularly, for example, by looking at whether a particular individual had built a sustainable pipeline of innovation that drove business results.

5. How is the system designed to be agile? Some of our systems tend to be rigid, and the processes to change goals or targets may be tedious. Agility or flexibility does not mean that you complete the year and then say, 'Hey, I did different things than what I planned to at the beginning of the year, so let me change my objectives!' That could lead to issues of governance! But yes, having a quarterly or half-yearly cadence of conversations and reviews and aligning goals, as required, during these conversations would make the process more relevant. In a more dynamic environment or in start-ups, having such a conversation every month would help. But the key is to step back and take a look at this objectively, and to do that, I recommend that we plan time for such regular reviews.

6. But the most important question we need to answer is this—at the end of the day, do people have clarity on what they should focus on? A simple test would be to ask them what their three priorities for the organization are and gauge how well they are able to articulate their answer. This needs a lot of communication. Current research shows that the clarity on the company's purpose and goals helps engagement, much more so among the younger population. The importance of creating a ritual around communicating the key priorities cannot be overemphasized. It is a great occasion to get people together, just to create a common understanding of what the organization is aiming for. Such events bring optimism, and are critical as we need to mobilize the commitment of our people. In large organizations, this is also an opportunity to showcase what is happening in different parts of the company. In the mid-'90s, Unilever wanted to build more synergies across different countries and move to a more global approach, and one of the key phrases that was used to build a burning platform for people to come together was 'If only Unilever knew what Unilever knows!' That equally applies to large companies now, a kind of 'not invented here' syndrome exists where every team wants to feel that they are the original thinkers behind an idea! We have all seen this across businesses or regions or countries, haven't we? Therefore, these annual events can be good times to communicate about our priorities but also to signal key behaviours needed.

Therefore, if you want to ensure that the expected results are achieved, you would have to make the choices amongst these:

Table 3
Continuum of Choices

Sustaining momentum (focus on operational goals)	Shifting the trajectory (transformational objectives)
No company/ business goals at the individual level	Company goals as a key part of individuals goals
A set template of standard goals	Flexible individual goals
Fixed goals	Agile approach to reviewing and changing goals
Limited communication	Communication and engagement at the core

At the end, your choices would depend on your business context and what you want to achieve. The nature of your business, the maturity stage of the organization and your strategic focus, would inform the choices you make, which could vary across groups. As a start-up, you would, of course, have an agile approach to reviewing and resetting goals periodically, and have more transformational goals for your leaders, while for your sales team, you need to have a very clear template of set objectives. Let me give the example of Swiggy, one of our unicorns. They decided that some policies will be different for different groups of people, moving away from standardization. The performance management process for their technology team was different from others. For instance, they created Swiggy Labs, a team that works on new ideas, takes them to 'proof of concept' and then to the market. They wanted a different DNA of people here, and their performance management is not linked to specific goals. They have three levels of people in these labs—creator, crafter and counsellor—and their salaries are completely linked to the market and not determined by any level. Also, any promotion in their technology team is not based on tenure. For a few key roles in technology, they have been exploring self-nomination for promotion, where a neutral body looks for critical evidence of the candidate's competencies based on their skill dictionary.

But my experience is that this can be an all-encompassing process, taking too much time and attention of the leadership, if we aim to get into too much control. However, use this exercise more to mobilize people, and build the emotions of optimism and pride, as those emotions are critical to get people to go the extra mile. Research tells us that when you want people to drive change and take up ambitious goals, they would do it when there are strong collective emotions of optimism and pride. In the end, that's what we need to create.

G. Raghavan, former global chief executive of NIIT's B2C training business, and currently CEO of Bhartiya City, a privately held real estate company, had remarked:

> People perform when the goals are clear, unambiguous, measurable and they themselves are empowered. While many organizations do this, they invariably fail to make the goals live on a daily basis. One of the great examples of 'presencing' the goals is NIIT's system of a perspective plan, a monthly operations review, a quarterly review and the mid-year strategic review. In all these reviews, both actions to be taken, and the results, were discussed in great detail against the plans agreed. What is more, the balanced score card and the performance rating and variable pay were rendered

totally objective with a small elbow room for subjective/team evaluation. Many companies may do this, but what is important is making this a culture. You could have walked into any of the 1,000 NIIT centres and asked the centre head to pull out the month's goals/year's goals and where she/he was that day and you will get a printout from the system—with not just the end financial numbers, but the goals in a kaleidoscope of variables that drive the business results!

So far, we talked of this whole process of objectives as it applies to leaders. But what about the others in the organization? As a practice, it is good to have some goals and targets for all, though at other levels it would be more operational goals. However, this is where I see big changes happening. The younger people entering the workforce increasingly want more autonomy and recognition as individuals. Therefore, here are a set of practices we should try:

1. In addition to a set of operational goals, it is a great practice to get them to work on one or two key projects of their interest. This is similar to a custom that 3M/Google adopted—do whatever you want for some part of your time, say 15–20 per cent of the time.[5] These projects serve as a development opportunity, yet they can tap into the creativity of the younger workforce.
2. Similarly, team goals are another interesting phenomena where a particular task requires a team to come together to deliver. This is ideal for project-based organizations or teams.
3. Job crafting is another practice gaining ground. In

concept, you add certain bits (a project or a different activity) to the job which is of real interest to the individual, and have non-standard goals for that part.

4. We would also have more gig workers in the future and much more remote work as many organizations move to a WFA mode. This would entail a greater focus on getting inputs and views from users and internal customers. I recommend that we focus on output metrics, with a lot of user feedback or a multi-stakeholder feedback system.

I guess these are some ways to engage the minds and hearts of the younger people entering the workforce. Many of these are not new; individual managers may have practised them with their teams. But we need to think of making these a part of every workplace and move directionally in terms of recognizing individuals, their interests and their development.

The Sting in the Tail?

Well, is this all that is needed to ensure the business achieves the results planned? No, there is one more all-important piece to close the loop. It is about how we evaluate the achievement and performance. That, in a way, determines how people respond to this whole process of going from strategy to action—the proverbial 'sting in the tail!'. While there are reams and reams written on the science of whether we need performance ratings, the bell curves, performance differentiation, and so on, in the end we have to keep it simple and go back to the basics. What is the outcome expected of us?

The key outcome we need is this: at the end of the period, the individual should know how she or he has performed against the set objectives. Some objective performance data is important, but more importantly it is the feedback on what she did well and the areas she could focus on in the future. The second outcome needed is for the organization to have some form of a record of performance for the future, and an objective and credible way to link that to rewards. We have to meet these outcomes in a way that keeps people motivated, and the performance focus of the business continually sharpened. To summarize, ask yourself these four questions:

1. Does the individual know how she performed and her strengths and areas to focus on?
2. Does the organization have a credible way to record the individual's performance and link this to rewards in a fair way?
3. Is the execution focus of the organization strengthened?
4. Are people feeling energized for the future?

Based on each of our business contexts, we could decide what is the best way forward. However, a lot of new research from positive psychology and neuroscience points to the fact that we need to move away from judging people's potential from limited data and buttonholing them in narrow buckets of performance. Acknowledgment of the strengths they bring and how they can leverage those would help, and our systems should be designed to look at these nuances.

Another idea is to do a blended rating of performance and behaviour descriptors. This creates a holistic rating, but needs good managerial judgement to assess the behaviours. You have performance and behavioural descriptors, and use these to rate people on the two scales and then use the blended rating. Whether you need ratings or not, there are many schools of thought, from which you can make a choice on the basis of your context. Some organizations are moving away from ratings and they have substituted it with a form of proxy performance indicator. The key is to have a credible way to communicate about the performance and strengths of the individual and link it to rewards.

As leaders, we have to visualize and put together the whole execution architecture. And, the key to that are the messages we send, our intent and focus. First, articulate your philosophy of execution clearly. You need to emphasize the sanctity of the goals, and yet be open to changing contexts and challenges. One of the traps I have seen companies fall into is inconsistency. It is important to have a coherent and consistent view on this. We then need to support execution with regular supportive conversations and some formal reviews. Building mechanisms for getting people to work together on cross-silo teams in an agile manner helps solve big, multidisciplinary problems. In Airtel, we started something called 'commando teams'—empowered teams that worked on key cross-functional projects and reported to the leadership team regularly. That helped get focus on key projects that required people from multiple functions. Lastly, we need to ensure that our recognition system is closely tied to the goals we want to achieve. So, in my mind, the four key leadership must-dos to build the execution architecture for the outcomes we need are as follows:

1. Articulate your philosophy of execution and performance clearly and be consistent.
2. Remove the friction to performance; this will come through regular conversations.

3. Enable mechanisms to accelerate cross-functional projects.
4. Align the reward and recognition systems appropriately.

◆

Sanjay Kapoor, former CEO of Bharti Airtel, currently an entrepreneur, TMT Advisor, independent board member and investor in multiple start-ups has the following insights:

Execution is at the heart of any business. But it needs to be tailored to the business context—the 'how' and 'what' we do would need to vary with the situation and structure. Let me explain with three scenarios that I have personally experienced.

At inception, we inherited a very public sector type model. License areas became operating telecom circles, spectrum allocation, circle classification, licenses conditions, KPIs and reporting, based on how state owned telecom operated and what the government wanted. Once the industry structure changed from duopoly to oligopoly, Airtel saw the execution opportunity and drove it by empowering these circles. We over-resourced them with a CEO, a COO, Marketing Head, Sales Head, HR and Finance, and managed them for growth only through a three-line graph: revenues, capex productivity and opex efficiency. We used a balanced scorecard to evaluate the circles. Many of the circles soon grew to be billion dollar organizations and our mobile revenue share shot up from circa 23.5 per cent to 32.5 per cent. We set the roll-out pace on execution for the industry!

Speaking of the competitive phase in 2010–13, Kapoor observed:

This was the time when telecom industry was moving from an oligopoly to hyper competition. On one hand, we had to protect our top-line and bottom-line and on the other, we had to grow from a 100 million to 200 million-customer base, in a belligerent price-war afflicted by the challengers. We knew that we have to execute well over the next two to three years to retain our market leadership, thought leadership, grow our business and transform it from voice to data. We changed tack. The focus of the circles, our operating unit, was shifted to operational excellence, singularly. We strengthened the functions at the centre and hired more powerful leaders in areas like marketing, customer experience, digital services and new revenue streams. 'Non-native' capabilities had to be hired and the 'social engine' had to be rewired to get this focus on operational excellence—different profiles of leaders, performance management focused on growth of revenue market share, customer experience and aligned rewards. This led to retaining our leadership position in a hyper competitive market, transformation from 2G to 3G/4G related services, creation and agglomeration of new businesses—DTH, Airtel Online, Airtel Money, Entertainment, Data Centres and our foray into Sri Lanka and Bangladesh.

Speaking about the current start-up ecosystem he says:

The best start-ups I see have a much longer term view of people and performance. But many are awash with short-term valuation pressure, and are busy dressing up the bride! What would help them is being much more thoughtful on what they are going to do with each individual in the organization, what they can expect from him/her and how they will measure their performance. That helps in bringing discipline to execution. Most start-up promoters find it hard to let go and take pride in how hard they work. Many can't sense when and how much room to create for professionals. The execution success in high growth start-ups is a function of how many more, truly capable, promoter like leaders you can create and keep them glued with respect and dignity, wealth creation and empowerment.

◆

To summarize, amongst the many important levers of execution, the ability to judge your situation and tailor your execution strategy to the business context; getting right people to do the right jobs; doing fewer things to perfection; focus and discipline; aligning your social engine and empowering people, are the elixir of my execution tool kit.

Key Takeaways

- Effective execution is at the heart of every successful business. Each organization has to find the right 'secret sauce', which suits their context, for execution. At the heart of execution are the concepts of management by objectives, as articulated by Peter Drucker.
- The first step is to: identify the key initiatives or focus areas that will help achieve your strategy. Clearly articulate and communicate these. Focus on not more than three to four key focus areas for a year.
- There are operational goals (for sustaining momentum) and there are transformational objectives (for shifting the curve). Depending on your business context and the type of roles, you could choose a balance of operational and transformational objectives. Do focus on at least a couple of transformational objectives for the leaders.
- There are other choices to make too. You have to balance between overall company or unit goals versus individual goals. You also have to make a choice whether you would have a set of fixed, cascaded objectives or more individualized, flexible objectives. All this would depend on your business context and approach to execution.
- Finding various ways to consistently communicate the priorities of the organization is critical. This empowers people down the line.
- The future could be about more agile goal-setting processes, with team goals. As we see more gig workers and WFA, focus could be on clear output

metrics plus a good system of user feedback or 180-degree feedback.

- The way people are evaluated for performance has a big impact on how you execute strategy and get results. While there has been a move to a rating-less system, using data and analytics, we still need to design a relevant system for each business context keeping these key elements in mind—
    a. Provide useful feedback to the employee
    b. Build a credible method to record performance improvement
    c. Link to rewards and energize people
    d. Ensure execution focus

References

1. Larry Bossidy and Ram Charan, with Charles Burck, *Execution: The Discipline of Getting Things Done*, Random House, 2011.
2. Peter F. Drucker, *The Practice of Management*, Harper Business, 2006.
3. Peter F. Drucker, *The Effective Executive: The Definitive Guide to Getting the Right Things Done*, Harper Business, 2006.
4. John Doerr, *Measure What Matters: OKRs-the Simple Idea That Drives 10x Growth*, Portfolio Penguin, 2018.
5. Vijay Govindarajan and Srikanth Srinivas, 'The Innovation Mindset in Action: 3M Corporation', *Harvard Business Review*, 6 August 2013, https://hbr.org/2013/08/the-innovation-mindset-in-acti-3. Accessed on 20 October 2021.

8

You Should Be Dancing

Driving Right Behaviours for Success

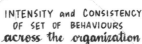

"CLEARLY OBSERVABLE or EXPERIENCED BEHAVIOURS, CONSISTENT OVER TIME."

INTENSITY and CONSISTENCY OF SET OF BEHAVIOURS *across the organization*

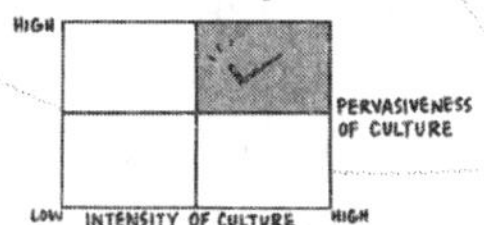

1. **ARTICULATE** BEHAVIOURS YOU WOULD LIKE TO SEE

   ALIGN THIS WITH YOUR STRATEGY

2. TRANSLATE THIS INTO **SHARED LANGUAGE** FOR PEOPLE TO UNDERSTAND

   MAKE IT **CLEAR and SPECIFIC**—HIGHLIGHT CHANGES FROM THE PAST

3. **ELICIT LEADERSHIP COMMITMENT**—GET THEM TO LEAD THE CHANGE

   TRAIN MIDDLE MANAGERS—MAKE THEM CHAMPIONS OF CHANGE

4. **ALIGN SOCIAL ENGINE** OF YOUR ORGANIZATION TO BEHAVIOURS

   FOCUS ON **PEOPLE SYSTEMS**, ESPECIALLY THOSE OF PERFORMANCE AND REWARDS

Sketchnote: Tanmay Vora

Driving the right behaviours is a critical outcome, the one that CEOs and leaders need to spend most time on. More so in a start-up. Getting the right behaviours in the organization for success cannot be copied easily. Hence, they are a critical source of competitive advantage.

If there is one company in India that can claim to have created a significant pool of CEOs and leaders, it is Hindustan Unilever (HUL), or its old avatar Hindustan Lever Ltd. But this did not happen by accident. It involved years of building the right behaviours in the organization, right from the time Unilever decided to appoint its first Indian CEO, Prakash Tandon, in 1961.

At Hindustan Unilever, where I worked for over two decades, we used to have a ritual called confirmation interviews. At the end of your graduate (management) training or your probation period, you would have to meet the chairman and could only be confirmed after that. The chairman, A.S. Ganguly, was an extremely respected but also a much-feared person. He was known to have turned down the confirmation of a few people. This confirmation meeting was also a kind of appraisal of your bosses as leaders, and they didn't want to be seen in a bad light in the confirmation interviews. So my factory manager had a couple of rounds of discussions with me and primed me up.

My confirmation interview was looming. I came from my factory the day before my interview that was scheduled for noon the next day. Before the interview with the Chairman, I had to meet Mr Keki Dadiseth, who was the personnel director those days. So, a bit apprehensive, I trundled up the stairs to the fifth floor to first meet him. Keki came out of his room, saw me and escorted me inside. He saw me sitting rigid and first asked me if the air conditioning was too cold for me. Then he did a bit of small talk about when I had came to Mumbai, his plan to visit our factory and how I was finding my job. This calmed my nerves. He then said, 'Come, let me take you to meet Dr Ganguly.' He walked me to Dr Ganguly's room, and then went inside first to meet him. He came back beaming and said, 'Good luck'. I was now confident; I felt like I had Keki's support. And my interview with Dr Ganguly went very well. He asked me about the factory and the key priorities in my work and, finally, I got confirmed as a manager!

This is just a small personal story, but it shows some elements of the secret behind the company's ability to develop so many leaders. They were, the commitment of the CEO and leaders, sacrosanct processes and a set of key behaviours that everyone in the company demonstrated. The seriousness with which the company took leadership development reverberated throughout the organization. It started from extreme focus on selecting the right people, with leaders spending significant time on it. A lot of attention was paid to the management training scheme, where each of the various stints were clearly articulated and the leaders spent substantial time with trainees, contacting them in the field and mentoring them.

The leaders perpetrated the abundance mentality as they knew that they had to develop successors and move on to other roles that might become available within HUL or Unilever, and they took immense pride in developing young people to take their roles. They gave time and importance to talent discussions and giving young managers a well-rounded experience through carefully planned career moves.

They showed willingness to bet on young talent and give them big jobs that would stretch and develop them. These were some of the key features that helped in creating this culture of talent development—a set of behaviours and actions that leaders consistently displayed, helping them to get the outcome they wanted. So how did HUL get all its people to consistently display these behaviours? How did they create this culture?

Whenever we speak of a 'culture', there are a couple of things that stand out. It is about clearly observable or experienced behaviours, consistent over time. Ideally, we also measure how pervasive these behaviours are in the organization and the intensity with which it is experienced. In a way, this is all in a continuum, you can have various shades. However, a strong, differentiating culture is one that is marked by greater intensity and consistency of a set of observed behaviours, and which is pervasive across the organization, setting it apart from others. The figure below, adapted from O'Reilly and Chatman's work on culture,[1] captures this:

Pervasiveness of the culture		
High	*Very pervasive but of low intensity* (*table stakes*)	*Highly pervasive and of high intensity* (*true differentiating culture*)
		High intensity but not pervasive (*a subculture*)
Low	Intensity of the culture	High

So, to go back to our core outcome expected, how do we get our people to demonstrate the right behaviours needed for success? To enable us to do that, we have to ask ourselves these five questions.

The first question you need to answer is 'what are those behaviours that are critical to our business success and will build a differentiated competitive advantage for us?' And this is where the choice of leadership plays a part. You can't be great at everything. The first is to look at your overall strategy and your core capabilities needed to be successful. The behaviours needed have to be the outcome of the core capabilities you need to build. For a consumer marketing company, it could be about being great at consumer insights and innovation that leads you to some specific behaviours. For a services company, it could be about customer/client focus, execution excellence and relevant behaviours. For instance, I am struck by the beliefs in the army—the commitment to never leave a fallen comrade behind. It assures people that they can depend on their colleagues to do the right thing when the time comes. This is a great example of relentless focus on teamwork and trust.

This becomes all the more important as organizations try to transform and also sharpen their performance. At this time, it will be a good exercise to think of what the new direction should be, and what behaviours would be needed for success. When Unilever embarked on its transformation in mid 2000s from many local brands to a set of global brands and a global brand development organization, it involved a key behaviour change, from being very local to becoming more global and working closely in a globally integrated organization. Most business transformations need a culture change to be successful—a set of new behaviours needed to enable and drive that change. When a new CEO takes over, this is one exercise she must do:

1. First, identify the key shifts in strategy, especially on 'how we will win'.
2. Identify two to three key behaviours that are essential for the strategy to be successfully implemented.
3. Take stock of the current culture—'what are those behaviours that we are consistently good at?' Listen to people with empathy, hear them talk about their successes and frustrations.
4. Understand which behaviours need to be retained and which ones need to be avoided. Understand how to leverage existing strengths of your culture.
5. Integrate and leverage the current strengths of the organization to what is needed for the future.

However, there is a danger at this stage: it could be too broad and amorphous. It would be useful to be a little sharper. A good way is to test if people can understand what specific behaviours or changes they need.

Another key point to remember is that sometimes we may need a behaviour change that is not linked to a strategy, but to some significant change you are bringing within the organization. For instance, as a major departure from your earlier system, you are launching a new performance development system in your organization by eliminating performance ratings. This would call for huge behaviour changes amongst people, especially managers. Take another example: you are making big changes to your sales incentive plans. Yes, follow the same methodology, as all of these need significant behaviour change to be successful.

The second question we need to ask is, 'do people know what they should be doing differently?' Clarifying it in simple terms and communicating it consistently is essential. There have been great examples of global organizations doing that. For instance, GE under Jack Welch got this new focus on execution excellence and cutting bureaucracy that led to the Six Sigma exercise and the Workout principles.[2] Repetition of those messages is essential to let people know what is expected of them. It is also essential to get the rationale, the 'why we are doing this', quite clear. Coherence is critical. Again, anything more than two to three key behaviour shifts will be lost on people, so it's important to keep it sharp and simple. A great example is Microsoft, which under the new CEO Satya Nadella, wanted to create a culture of collaboration and get people to adopt a growth mindset.[3]

I have found that we need to translate this at three levels, because each has a clear role to play:

1. First is to shift the mindset of people, telling them what is important to the leadership and why. This needs to be broad and inspiring, with a solid 'reason to believe' to capture the attention of people. For instance, Microsoft communicated that they would like to move from 'know it all' to 'learn it all' mindset. That's a powerful way to communicate.[4] The 'why' this is important should come out very clearly, and should be coherent to all.
2. The second level is to ensure that these behaviours reflect in what you might use to assess and develop people—maybe competencies or any set of standards. This needs to be a little more detailed in terms of specific behaviours expected. For instance, the same 'learn it all' behaviour might be detailed

as being open to diverse points of view, being curious, learning from others (including parts of the organization) and building on them, experimenting and trying new ideas and upskilling oneself. At this level, it helps people understand the behaviours at a more specific level.

3. The third level is what I call 'decision tiebreaker'. This reinforces what people should choose in key moments of truth or when under pressure. For instance, things like the 'customer is always right' or the 'if in doubt, decide on what will help the customer' are examples that help people prioritize actions when faced with tough choices.

In the end, we have to remember three key principles in defining the behaviours for a culture change. Keep it focused, keep it simple and make it coherent. I can't stress on this enough, but these are very critical when we need to articulate behaviour changes needed—focus, simplicity and coherence. We need to create a shared language, clarity on the intent as well as the behaviours expected.

The third question would be, 'is my leadership committed to this change?'

If there is one lever for behaviour change that far outweighs others, it is the commitment and sponsorship of the leadership. Research shows that this has twice the impact of any lever on behaviour change.[5]

It starts with the business leader who needs to walk the talk! The leader should visibly focus on three to four areas that mean a lot to people and demonstrate by actions. The key platforms for the CEO are the annual strategy meet, the regular monthly or quarterly business reviews, key appointment or promotions of people, town halls, 'all-hands' meet, internal awards and recognitions, etc. Each of these can be significant platforms to signal the new behaviours. Research shows that modelling of the behaviours by the leaders is extremely critical and builds momentum. When people are not sure of what to do, they copy the actions of others, especially those with power and status.

But a CEO alone cannot drive behaviour change in an organization. I have seen examples of CEOs trying to get changes done without the full buy-in of the leadership, and it invariably goes nowhere. Leadership commitment is important because every employee looks up to his or her leader, and if they see them living the new behaviours, they know it is serious. If the leaders don't practice it, we can bid goodbye to the new behaviours. Get your leaders on board. They should champion the new behaviours needed. The key to getting leaders on board is to get them to be part of the process of identifying the new behaviours needed and making them take on key roles to make the change happen.

In addition to the leaders, we need to get key influencers at all levels of the company to evangelize and champion the new behaviours. There are network analysis tools that help you identify your key influencers and it would be essential to make them your ambassadors for the behaviour change.

The fourth question you ask yourself is this: 'Are all my HR systems aligned to support the new behaviours?'

Behaviours are enabled and reinforced by the social systems architecture that we design. The implicit and explicit nudges drive those behaviours and habits. How do we assess people? How do we promote people? How do we recognize them? How do we reward them? How do we develop them? How do we hire and move them? What do we incentivize?

Let's go back to the Microsoft example. When Satya

Nadella announced the need to be more collaborative, one of the actions the company undertook was to change the performance management. They practised a five-point rating system for performance, with some quotas. Top performers were hoarded and those who rated lower would not be able to find other internal opportunities. They changed that to a system which now looked at performance across three dimensions—your own individual accomplishments in the business, your contributions to the success of others and your results that build on the work or ideas of others. This is a key change intended to help collaboration across the organization.

Very often, we don't look at the overall social architecture before we plan changes in behaviour. As you know, we are prisoners of our habits. Our behaviours are our habits reinforced over time by all the social systems in the organizations. Changes in the social systems have a multiplier effect too. First, they help move to the new behaviour. Second, they signal that you are serious about it.

There are many cases where our social systems play an implicit role. In one organization I worked in, we launched an internal job posting (IJP) system but didn't find many takers. On closer analysis, we found that people did not apply for an IJP three to four months before the annual performance cycle as they felt they would lose out on their performance being recognized. Second, they thought that this whole process was fixed. They didn't want to risk going to another region/unit but bide their time in the existing team till an opportunity came up there. So the issue was clearly with the performance system and how people were being promoted. Unless we made changes to those, we would not create the right behaviours to enable internal mobility.

I was speaking to a colleague in the fashion apparel industry and he quoted the example of Inditex group (which owns the brand Zara), one of the world's largest retailers where they say the word 'impossible' does not exist. Zara has a very entrepreneurial culture, and employs lots of young talent who quickly climb through the ranks of the company. They promote approximately two-thirds of their store managers from within and generally experience a low turnover. The brand has no fear in giving responsibility to young people and the culture encourages risk-taking (as long as learning happens) and fast implementation (the mantra of fashion). The leadership gives its store managers full liberty and control over their store's operations and performance, with clearly set cost, profit and growth targets, with a fixed and variable compensation scheme reflecting Zara's commitment to talent development. This is evident in their leadership values of teamwork, open communications and self-imposed high-standards that lead to a clear direction and guidance for their employees and the organization as a whole.

Another interesting example of building a culture of risk taking is in Oyo. They would identify a leader to explore a market, hire a team and take ownership in developing that business. The leadership tells the team not to worry about making mistakes and encourages it to correct it on the way. People, therefore, take pride in having built a business. Moreover, Oyo encourages people to invest in other start-ups, and leaders are actively encouraged to mentor other founders and start-ups. All of this helps build a culture of entrepreneurship and risk taking.

Similarly, Flipkart creates 'pods' of people to solve business problems. They get the internal employees to pitch their ideas (in the customary start-up spirit) to help

Flipkart grow their business and other employees could join a particular idea that they find interesting and work on it.

The last question for you is this: 'how do I know we are moving in the right direction? And how do I sustain this?'

Behaviours and habits take time. Realize that it is a journey. We have to enable employees and remove any friction in moving to the new behaviours. Constantly keep looking for the right behaviours and recognizing them, tracking their progress closely over time.

Here are the three key areas we need to focus on. To get people to adopt the new behaviours, the first step is to get them to experiment with it. Focus on removing any friction to adopting the new behaviour. Provide a safe environment for them to try the new behaviours. A great way to ensure compliance as people learn new habits is to create a checklist. That will help them avoid missing out on any new steps and also enable others to call out any slippage.[6] For instance, when you launch a new sales process, a checklist of actions would help people start those new behaviours. Learning from the research on habits, use cues and triggers to get people to adopt new behaviours and make the first step an easy one. Early incentives for adopting behaviours definitely help. A small token incentivizes people to take those first steps. Giving slight nudges to get people to take that first step is critical. Try and add the new behaviours to something they love doing, what scientists are now calling 'habit-stacking'.[7]

Recognizing early adopters and celebrating small wins help build momentum and creates energy. The CEO/leaders should take time to recognize people who are demonstrating the new behaviour and showcase them. Getting teams to celebrate their small success in the new ways of working empowers them and drives them to continue on the new path.

And finally, identify the outcomes you expect from the new behaviour, in addition to the specific behaviours you want to see demonstrated. While the outcomes will have a lag effect and take time to show up, the behaviours can be tracked in terms of a regular employee survey where you could check on the behaviours exhibited or visible actions that can be measured.

But there is one critical insight we need to keep in mind as we talk of change. This comes from one of the masters in this field, Kurt Lewin. He articulated this concept of force field analysis, and spoke of the driving forces (those pushing for the change)[8] and the restraining forces (those resisting change). Imagine a plank of wood held by two springs, one on top, which is the driving force, and the one at the bottom, which is the restraining force, holding the plank at equilibrium. Now, there are two ways to make change happen: you increase the strength of the driving force, so the spring on top exerts more pressure, and the spring at the bottom is at greater tension and compressed. You will get change, but you can see the tension in the bottom spring, and that change will not be sustainable. It is far easier to drive change by removing the restraining forces, by relaxing that spring at the bottom. Remove the friction, reduce the causes of resistance and that will lead to sustainable change. Let's add one more insight from behavioural science to this, called 'endowment effect'. This simply means that people attach a greater value to things they own or possess. That's why there is a big resistance if people have to give up something they enjoyed or possessed. They place a lot more value to what they have, compared to what they don't own or possess. This understanding is critical in managing change.

Unilever split its business into two groups in 2001—foods

and home and personal care.[9] The foods business in Asia was headed by Louis 'Tex' Gunning, a Dutch Unilever Foods veteran. To grow the foods business, he felt the company has to deeply understand the habits of local people so the company could develop relevant local foods other than the tea and margarine which were Unilever's mainstays. He also wanted to create a community of foods people who would be passionate about growing the foods business. 'Build Asian Food Business for Asians by Asians' was the objective. Unilever had just completed a merger with Bestfoods and there was need to integrate and get the team together.

To do so, he planned a series of 'journeys' where people from across Unilever Foods Asia would spend a few days deeply interacting with the local population. The first journey was planned in Guilin in China where the 150 odd people from Foods Asia spent a couple of days with local people—the fishermen, the factory workers, the orchard workers, etc. and reflected upon their aspirations and challenges. The next journey was in India where teams of people visited almost 25 NGOs or charities and spent a few days there, for instance in the Golden Temple, in Mother Teresa's Sisters of Charity, etc. and looked at what made the community work. The following year, the team spent a week in Sri Lanka post the tsunami, helping with rehabilitation work for a couple of days, also understanding the people and their challenges. Of course, all of these exercises need to be backed with facilitation and reflections.

What these journeys did was two-fold. First, it helped build a community of people in Foods Asia, and ignited in them the passion and desire to grow foods. This was also an opportunity for the people to connect with each other and learn what others were doing. Second, it brought people closer to the local communities in various countries, increasing sensitivity to the local needs. That also brought about more dignity and respect for the local communities and a greater understanding of the food needs. Finally, it was about building the right leadership mindset.

This is what **Jackie Koh,** who was the SVP HR for Unilever Foods Asia at the time, had to say on these journeys:

> The journey was a metaphor for our top 100 leaders to delve into the issue of leadership. We advocated: leadership is a choice, not an anointment. Our leaders were posed the questions, 'who am I?', 'who are we as a community?' and 'what is our raison d'être as a Foods business?' The Foods business required new people, a food mindset and a new corporate culture which could inspire our leaders to take on the knocks of a new business and pull punches above their weight. We realized that self-determination was key. Accordingly, the journeys were designed to encourage introspection to determine personal values, thereby creating more meaning at work. We encouraged them to design their destinies and to adopt growth mindsets—from workplace to communities, minor in size to major in determination, from start-up to legacy-building.
>
> We started with leadership teams of the 13-odd countries and inspired them to go beyond typical communications to create inspiring movements instead. The collective was always emphasized to encourage larger boundaries, more sharing, diversity and adaptive thinking-action.

This is one example of how one can build a common identity and get an entire group of people to behave differently.

Anand Kripalu, former CEO, Diageo India and current MD and Global CEO of EPL Ltd, led the transformation of the company after United Spirits was acquired by it over seven years ago. He has had a stellar career with Unilever spanning over 22 years and then as CEO of Mondelez India and South East Asia. Here are some insights, in his own words, on how he led the transformation of behaviours amongst people:

When we started this integration, one of the first things we did was to get together as a leadership team and discuss what kind of a company we wanted. That's the first step. Most often people don't have a clear vision of what they want to build. Therefore, ask yourself, 'Can I see the company I want to build in my mind?'

We then translated that into a set of variables or behaviours as we moved on from being a promoter led company. Some of the key elements that we defined were:

1. Non-hierarchical
2. Apolitical
3. Performance and merit based
4. Open and transparent
5. Compliant

This was a big shift from what the company was used to. So the first step was to get the leadership aligned to this. People see how you behave and how you operate. The behaviours in the larger organizations are often a reflection of how the CEO and the leadership team behave.

Some small but powerful symbolic changes bring out the messages loud and clear. For instance, we abolished the reserved elevators for senior management and the reserved parking. We also created open offices. This was done consciously to emphasize that we will be more open and non-hierarchical.

But it wasn't all smooth sailing. We had people who didn't live up to these standards. We have separated with people on compliance grounds because they didn't take us seriously. The 'how' you achieve results is equally important to 'what' you achieve. I have personally had hour-long conversations with a high performer who surpassed his numbers, but did not exhibit the right behaviours. It is not easy, but you need to do it. We have docked bonuses and performance ratings of people just because they didn't demonstrate the right behaviours, the right leadership standards and didn't live up to the right culture.

Communication is critical. We have town halls where we discuss case studies of people who do not exhibit the right behaviours.

We have to make sure people know what is expected, and how serious we are about it. I truly believe that culture is the only sustainable source of competitive advantage. The right culture attracts top talent. Our focus on the right culture and inclusion has also enabled us to make women comfortable to work here. In our top 50 leaders, we now have nearly one-third women, with 40 per cent women in our executive committee. This was done by driving this hard, but also with a lot of training on inclusion, on bias, etc. And it was not easy in the alcohol industry. When we started the integration, this was a man's industry. We had to position ourselves as ethical marketeers of alcohol, and to do that we had to take some tough calls. We had a brand called 'Diet Mate' which people thought was good for weight management! We killed that brand. We have given breathalyzers to the police to stop drunk-driving and encourage responsible consumption of alcohol. Now we can proudly say that we are ethical marketeers.

My experience has clearly convinced me that culture is the most important thing a leader can build. That is the real legacy he or she can leave behind!

Key Takeaways

- Culture is about clearly observable or experienced behaviours, consistent over time. A strong, differentiating culture is one that is marked by greater intensity and consistency of a set of observed behaviours, which is pervasive across the organization, setting it apart from others.
- The first question is to articulate what behaviours you would like to see—this is critical. The more thought you give to this, and the more aligned this is with your strategy, the better the results.
- Next, we need to translate this into a shared language for people to understand easily. All your employees should know, in clear and specific terms, what they should be doing differently.

- The leadership team has twice the impact on any sustainable behaviour change in the organization. Get your leadership team committed to this first and get them to lead the change. This may also mean training middle managers and making them champions of change.
- Ensure that you align the social engine of your organization to the behaviour you need, the various people systems, especially those on performance and rewards.
- Habit formation takes time. Try and remove any friction for exhibiting the new behaviours. Use checklists and cues to get people to adopt new behaviours. Celebrate small wins and inculcate positive emotions like optimism and pride to build momentum.
- Change is more sustainable if we try to remove the restraining forces, rather than push through change. Due to the endowment effect, people place more value to what they already enjoy or possess, and hence there will be greater resistance if something is seen as being taken away. It may be easier to give alternate options, which people choose, rather than remove what they already have.

References

1. C. A. O'Reilly and J.A. Chatman, 'Culture as Social Control: Corporations, Cults, and Commitment,' in B.M. Staw and L. Cummings ed., *Research in Organizational Behaviour*,157–200, JAI Press, 1996.
2. 'Six Sigma Case Study: General Electric', Six Sigma, 22

May 2017, https://www.6sigma.us/ge/six-sigma-case-study-general-electric/. Accessed on 20 October 2021.

3. Ashley Stewart and Shana Lebowitz, 'Case Study: How Satya Nadella Overhauled Microsoft's Cutthroat Culture and Turned It into a Trillion-dollar "Growth Mindset" Company,' *Business Insider*, 4 March 2020, https://www.businessinsider.in/tech/news/case-study-how-satya-nadella-overhauled-microsofts-cutthroat-culture-and-turned-it-into-a-trillion-dollar-growth-mindset-company/articleshow/74466098.cms. Accessed on 6 September 2021.
4. 'Making Organizations More Human Through Science,' NeuroLeadrship, https://neuroleadership.com/. Accessed on 6 September 2021.
5. Boris Groysberg, Jeremiah Lee, Jesse Price and J. Yo-Jud Cheng, 'The Leader's Guide to Corporate Culture', *Harvard Business Review,* Issue: January–February 2018, https://hbr.org/2018/01/the-leaders-guide-to-corporate-culture. Accessed on 20 October 2021.
6. Atul Gawande. *The Checklist Manifesto: How to Get Things Right,* Penguin Books, 2014.
7. James Clear, *Atomic Habits: An Easy and Proven Way to Build Good Habits and Break Bad Ones*, Random House, 2018.
8. 'Force Field Analysis', Multi-Stakeholder Partnerships, Wageningen Centre for Development Innovation, http://www.mspguide.org/tool/force-field-analysis. Accessed on 20 October 2021.
9. CNN Staff, 'Unilever to Split Units', *CNN Money*, 4 August 2000, https://money.cnn.com/2000/08/04/europe/unilever/. Accessed on 20 October 2021.

9

Life in the Fast Lane

BUILDING LEADERSHIP AND SUCCESSION

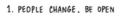

PRINCIPLES TO KEEP IN MIND FOR LEADERSHIP DEVELOPMENT

1. PEOPLE CHANGE, BE OPEN
2. CONTEXT and CIRCUMSTANCES PLAY A BIG ROLE
3. EVERYONE HAS THEIR SUPERPOWER, HARNESS IT
4. DON'T 'HARD-CODE' LABELS ON PEOPLE
5. LIFE SCARS TELL A STORY

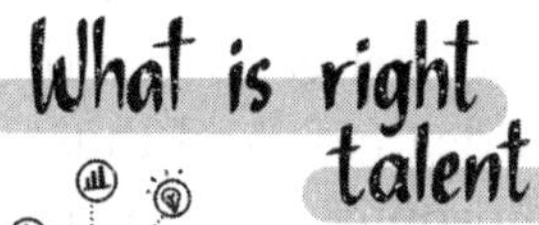

SKILLS, BEHAVIOURS, EXPERIENCES, MINDSET

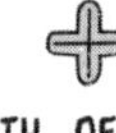

STRENGTH OF INTERNAL/ EXTERNAL NETWORK AS APPROPRIATE FOR ROLE

- USE VARIETY OF INPUTS TO IDENTIFY STRENGTHS
- BE WARY OF LABELING PEOPLE AS HIGH-POTENTIAL
- GET A BROAD IDEA OF TOP 15-20% TALENT FOR DEVELOPMENT

DEVELOPING TALENT

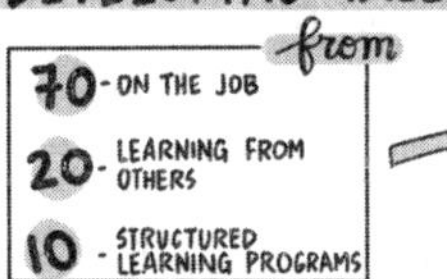

from
70 - ON THE JOB
20 - LEARNING FROM OTHERS
10 - STRUCTURED LEARNING PROGRAMS

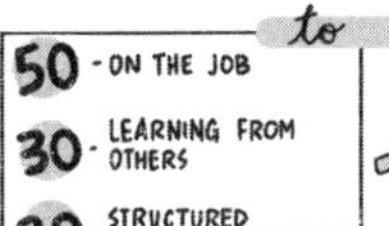

to
50 - ON THE JOB
30 - LEARNING FROM OTHERS
20 - STRUCTURED LEARNING PROGRAMS

IN A FAST-CHANGING WORLD, PEOPLE HAVE TO LEARN FROM A BROADER ECOSYSTEM

COACHING and MENTORING

Have more coaches who know the context

Develop more internal leaders who can adopt coaching style

CAREER PATHS

Provide a framework for more fluid, personalized, multi-directional career paths

the most strategic action → DEVELOPING FUTURE-FIT LEADERS

Many years ago, I was speaking to a group of senior HR folks at Unilever in London, after spending a full day in an assessment exercise to select graduates, and we got debating about milk rounds. I asked what the sense in hiring history and classical art graduates as management trainees was. Surely, Unilever would be better off hiring people with economics or business degrees. And thus, started a long discussion about the philosophy of management, the idea of leadership potential, who is the right leader and so on. That was truly an enriching conversation and gave me great insights. In every talent discussion that I have had since with many leaders, I have learnt a lot about leaders and leadership. Some of my assumptions and beliefs on leadership have changed over time.

However, my greatest insight after all these years is that the basic principles of leadership development have not changed, but the subtleties have become more acute. So in a way, it has become more nuanced and we can't use the broad brush any more. The world has changed, and is changing even more. Our concept of careers has changed—we are seeing many people pivot and move on to do different things in their 30–40 years of working life. We have also moved to an environment where there is abundance of opportunities for talent and greater access to it. The traditional Unilever way or the GE way, that worked so well in the '80s and '90s, may need to be tweaked for the new context. Moreover, my last few years working in a B2B services organization changed some of my original thinking on leadership development that was strongly fashioned by the large FMCG/industrial businesses. Context is critical. Deep continuing client relationships and industry expertise do matter. All of this points to some fundamental changes in the way we develop our leaders.

So let's go back to this foundational outcome—we have to ensure that we have the right leaders to drive the business and there is a pipeline of leaders. So the questions we need to answer are—who is the right leader? How do we find them? How do we build them? The fundamental intent here is to have 'future fit' talent so, in this fast-changing world, we need to develop people who will be the ideal fit to do big roles in the future.

Here are some basic principles that we need to be reminded of; we know them, but sometimes we lose sight of them, which leads us to inevitable biases.

1. **People change:** Every individual is constantly evolving; continuously learning; adapting to the stimulus around them, learning from the people around them. People who you may write off may do very well in a different environment. I have learnt this lesson many times. I felt a person working with me was a disaster but after ten years I found that the person was doing very well in a big global role in a different function. At the very core, this means leaders need to keep an open mind, and continuously look for new data on people.
2. **Context matters:** The role of the context in an individual's performance is oftentimes underrated. Of course, part of that context is what an individual creates, and hence deserves credit for. But in most cases, there are many extraneous influences that we need to be cognizant of when we look at people and their performance. The best is to see how people perform in different contexts. It also brings out their core strengths, but different contexts help them develop significantly.

Secondly, what kind of leadership development practices you will adopt depends on the organizational context and the maturity level that is constantly evolving.

3. **Everyone has a strength or a sweet spot:** Every individual has a set of core strengths, and our role should be to identify those and leverage them. We also have to apply the 'context lens' here—strength in one context may not be the same in another, so be sure it is a proven strength. What we should also look for are very strong derailers—those are the behaviours that trip people. There are always areas for people to develop which, over time, they would do with the right feedback and coaching. But these strong derailers are the ones that need very strong feedback early on and a close watch. For instance, over-ambition, lack of humility, not sharing credit with the team are all critical derailers.
4. **Don't hard-code labels:** One of my learnings, as a corollary from the first principle mentioned above (people change), is not to hard-code labels on people. Take, for instance, the identification of high-potentials. While it is important to have a sense of who are the ones you feel have the potential to take on bigger roles, so you can bet on them, don't 'hard-code' the label of high potential on them. Use them as broad guidelines, and constantly seek and be open to new insights on people This will help in getting a better understanding of the team.
5. **Life scars tell a lot more about people:** What drives people is critical. What are their deeper motives in life? Where are they from? What has made them who they are? What is their inner drive or motive? What kind of life scars do they have and how has it shaped them? We have

to understand people more deeply and realize that the life scars they may have had determined their behaviour and character. Digging a bit deeper than just the behaviours you observe, and understanding what drives them, is truly helpful. You may all have heard of the iceberg principle. We only see the individual's behaviours, but don't see their motives, values and what drives them. Significant life events and crucible experiences shape people, and it will help to get to know this better.

Those are my five basic principles to keep in mind as we try and look at how we plan to achieve our outcome of having the right talent in the key jobs and building a pipeline. We will try and answer each of the questions below.

The Right Talent

We saw earlier that you could describe talent in terms of skills, behaviours, experiences and mindset (the SBEM framework). Skills are about 'what' the individual can do, their expertise, and behaviours (or competencies in HR jargon) are about 'how' they get it done, their execution edge. Experiences are about what the individual has specifically done and built credibility in—the medals on their chest. These experiences give them credibility and a shorter runway to succeed in a similar role. For instance, a person would have led a couple of transformations in a business or turned around the business. Those kind of experiences matter if you want someone to scale up faster. The 'mindset' element is important. If you follow football, you may be familiar with attack-oriented midfielders or defensive-minded midfielders. What's their natural mindset?

Are they growth-oriented or more keen on sweating assets? Are they naturally internally process focused or externally customer focused? For critical executive (CXO) roles, the appropriate mindset becomes very important. The key point is that 'right talent' is defined by the role and the crucial challenges in the role at that point of time. For instance, at a point in time you may need a Chief Financial Officer (CFO) who needs to put stronger control systems, and at another point in time you may need a growth focused, risk-friendly CFO. So when you decide on the right talent, look at the context of the role, and then decide what is the right talent.

But there is more insight on this. In addition to the above, Boris Groysberg, in his research, came up with two other key elements for success in a role—strength of internal networks (including knowledge of internal systems/history), and strength of external networks.[1] There are some roles that need good internal networks, say HR, whereas some others don't need it, like in sales. In fact, in those roles, especially in a B2B industry, strength of external networks is crucial. These elements become important when you look at whether to hire external talent or build internally. Therefore, this equation helps us think about the right talent:

Right talent: f(Skills, Behaviours, Experiences, Mindset) for the particular context + strength of internal/ external networks (I/E) as appropriate for the role.

So what's next then? It will be a good idea to take stock of your current talent in all your key roles—you will have the objective performance data, and along with the above framework of SBEM+I/E, you could have a productive discussion. These questions could help:

1. Given the business context and current challenges for the role, what are the areas of concern, given the individuals and their performance?
2. What could be the future challenges in these roles, given the business trajectory and does this pose some questions?
3. How can those areas of concern be handled: by feedback or coaching, by additional support in terms of bolstering team, or by changing people?
4. Are there any changes/moves in talent to plan for? What might be good for their long-term development, and what would the business needs be?

My experience is that changing people, unless done as part of planned career development moves, costs time and effort. A new talent takes time to settle, and in senior roles almost six months to a year is lost in such surgical changes. Yes, they need to be done at times but after you have evaluated other options. Investing in development, therefore, is far more effective.

Another good practice is to have talent councils, which meet regularly to look into the talent needs of the future. For instance, if we have a functional council for finance, they may start thinking about how the role of the CFO may change in the future and implications for talent development now. Like the finance function looks at sources and applications of funds, these talent councils can take a strategic perspective of the sources and development and deployment of talent!

In my two-decade-long career in Unilever, one of the things that clearly stood out was the identification of high potentials. It was quite simple, in a way. You were put on the list as a high potential if they saw the leadership potential in you to move to the next level, and that's how high potentials came to be known as 'listers'. How did one get on this list? The official process those days was that if you showed significant strength in five out of the 11 'competencies' (demonstrated behaviour), along with higher performance, you could be proposed to be on the list. The business or functional leader took the final call on whether you could be a lister. In HUL, however, there used to be a 'functional resource committee'—a group of leaders in a function led by the functional head (the CFO for finance with all the finance heads in different businesses), who would discuss and agree.

Roughly about 15 per cent of the population was identified as listers across the company with, of course, a higher proportion in functions like marketing and lesser in manufacturing, etc. The listers had the benefit of a higher annual increment and got onto premier training programmes meant for the high potentials! A key measure that was tracked was our 'list cover', which was simply the number of listers identified at a level over the total number of positions at the next higher level. Taking the finance example, if we had eight positions at the VP level in a country and six people identified as 'listers' for the VP level, your list cover was 75 per cent.

This model worked well for over four decades, but a couple of years ago, Unilever moved out of this system of classifying people as listers. They probably felt it had outlived its utility. What could be some reasons that would have led to this? First, this concept of 'listers' or high potentials was seen to be non-inclusive, and against the philosophy that everyone had an equal chance to grow. Second, we are in an age where specialist knowledge is becoming more important, rather than just leadership potential.

This model of identifying hi-potentials and prioritizing development and career moves for them has also not been very successful in B2B companies. In these cases, since individual customer connect is more critical, that trumps other areas. I have seen people leading an account and growing with it for even a decade. So where specialization or customer relationships count, the high potential model is not easily applicable as these roles need unique skills and valued relationships. And, in an environment where there is a lot of change, you need to be the right person (with relevant SBEM) for the job at that time, irrespective of whether you have been labelled a high-potential or not.

For these reasons, organizations are moving away from the traditional nine-box matrix that we all swore by. Remember the performance potential grid? Let me rephrase this. Organizations are clearly moving away from a rigid application of high potential assessment and classifying people and communicating to them. However, using these models to identify people for key career moves or development projects is clearly recommended. Acceleration of key talent, and thus differentiation, is important and therefore we need to identify them. From the rigid, perception-based models of yore, various new talent models now pick up objective data on performance and behaviours, and help bring a picture of talent that can be used for decision-making on an ongoing basis.

Make it dynamic, get objective data and get multi-stakeholder perspectives. There are certain behaviours that are clearly indicative of potential to grow as a transformational leader, like the breadth of business view, dealing with uncertainty, ability to see patterns and to outline a bold strategic vision and mobilizing people. But it may not be relevant to label people on potential (like high potential, etc.), unless you have a robust proven mechanism. It is far more useful to categorize their development areas.

I have also found the benefits of running a formal development centre at key levels, especially big transition levels. Choose ones which are simulation based, where actual behaviour is observed. Substantiated with some other motive/strengths assessment and a 360-degree feedback, it helps get an objective view of talent. More importantly, it helps us give feedback to people that is much more development focused, and people are more open to it. One of the issues we deal with is that people don't give right feedback for various reasons. We spoke of derailers earlier; unless people get feedback on potential behaviours, which will sabotage their career, and then work on them, those behaviours will show up later and come in the way of a person's growth. Such development centres help provide a context for such feedback. However, you may not need a development centre where there is a regular process of multi-stakeholder feedback and regular talent discussions instituted in your organization.

To summarize, it is important to have some robust way of identifying talent who can be your future bet, or more correctly, the development areas for people who aspire for growth. The first option is a recommendation from the manager as a part of a process, supported by discussions with other leaders that have a perspective on talent. The second way is to have a mechanism of a development centre, along with manager feedback. Finally, the third way is to get a series of objective data on performance and behaviours, including 360-degree and regular manager and stakeholders perspective, and build a picture of talent. Choose whatever works for you, but at the heart of that should be these principles that you need to keep in mind:

1. Performance data is distinct from the potential data. Consistent high performance is important—it gives an indication of the relevant behaviours they may be demonstrating for that role. But, are the same behaviours relevant for a higher role? Behaviours and mindset are stronger indications of future potential, coupled with consistent high performance and skills. Outline which behaviours, in your organizational context, are clearly indicative of potential—it is possible you may have different behaviours for a strategic leadership role, like the head of a business or a marketing head, as opposed to a strong operating role.
2. Ensure you get multi-stakeholder perspective on behaviours, especially in the context of future challenges. For movement to significant leadership levels, getting an outside-in view of potential helps. For instance, Bosch has a practice of a detailed 'potential-oriented interviews', done by a specialist, which helps with inputs but more importantly, becomes very crucial to plan the development of the individual in the new role.
3. A key point here is the aspiration of individuals—some may want to grow in leadership roles, others may want something else. Clearly, the responsibility for career management is with the individual.
4. Be wary of labelling people on their potential. That is dynamic. Focus more on thinking about their development path.

Developing Future Leaders

There is a ton of literature on how we could develop future leaders and as many approaches. In the fast changing world, we will get the biggest leverage from the focus on development more than on assessment of talent. But if you want to ensure that you continually develop a pipeline of leaders, here are a few principles that we may have to keep in mind, building on things that have worked, and yet adding nuances due to the changing world.

- **The right set of assignments:** We all learn by actually doing our jobs, especially new things in our jobs—a new kind of project, a project that stretches thinking, a project that makes them reach out to other parts of the organization, etc. In my experience, this is the best way. It is part of everyday business, there is a true need and all we are doing is linking it to an individual's development. But this is very much dependent on the manager, and that's why, to make this successful, you need managers to take ownership and build this habit into their everyday work. Many of us have a lot of projects to do in our work. All we need to do is ask 'how can this project be a development opportunity for someone in my team?' Get each manager to link their key projects or assignments on how they can develop someone in their team. This will lead to institutional development.

  Many organizations have a well-established system of aligning business projects with leadership development, and getting their future leaders to work on key cross- functional, business-critical projects.

One example I heard was from Marico; their Young Board initiative. The Young Board is a cross-functional team comprising eight young leaders from different functions from Marico Global. This board works on identifying new opportunities, looking at potential pitfalls and provides recommendations on the initiatives identified. The board members are expected to wear the organizational hat and collaborate as a team of talented individuals to create and deliver the objectives of the assigned initiative, and it helps them build a strategic business perspective. Adecco has another interesting practice, what they call 'CEO for one month', where young leaders are selected after a rigorous process, and they get an opportunity to work with the global CEO for a month.

- **Coaching and mentoring:** At the basic level, it is about helping someone else be successful. Ideally, that should be the role of each manager—making each member of your team successful. Sir John Whitmore, who pioneered coaching in the '90s, defines it as 'unlocking people's potential to maximize their own performance'.[2] There are many ways in which we can help. It is actually a continuum between simple directions or advice (called mentoring) on one hand, to asking questions that make people reflect on their own actions and find their own solutions (non-directive coaching) on the other. So if I were to adapt Herminia Ibarra and Anne Scoular's classification of these helping relationships, we can plot them on two axis: one is the extent of 'expertise' that is put in by the 'helper', and the other is the extent it is owned and initiated by the 'helped' (they call this 'energy pulled out' but I find the ownership element more relevant, in fact it is the 'energy put in' by the helped).[3]

High Extent of expertise put in by the 'helper'	**High expertise, information provided, low ownership by the helped** (General expert advice, some mentoring would fall here)	**High expertise, high ownership by helped** (Coaching by leaders with great contextual knowledge of the situation)
	No growth zone!	**Low expertise provided, but greater ownership and work by the helped** (Listening, questioning, non-directive coaching)
Low	**Extent of energy put in by the 'helped'**	High

All types of such development conversations are relevant depending on the situation. As you can see, we should plan for all these types of interactions within an organization, and also train managers to do so. Managers are not naturally good at non-directive coaching, listening, asking questions, and that is one area we could train them. But make sure you design opportunities for employees for all these broad set of interactions: mentoring by seniors on work and career, non-directive coaching for big behavioural changes and situational coaching by the leaders.

There are key moments when each of these types of interactions becomes essential. For instance, when you hire fresh trainees into your organization, they will benefit from some general mentoring. Giving them a mentor or a guide for the first year is a wonderful way to develop them. When people transit into a new, bigger role, then a kind of transition coaching by the manager will help. Of course, the regular performance conversation should also be an expertise-led coaching conversation. Coaching people early on gives far more dividends than coaching a leader who thinks he has arrived. So, there are clearly three key actions. First, create an awareness of these different kinds of coaching situations and provide those opportunities to your teams. Second, enable people, train them to be good at these different ways. Finally, and most importantly, as leaders, you set the example. You need to walk the talk, show that you value these, which then prompts others to do similarly and build a virtuous cycle.

Shadowing is another good way to broaden perspective. One of the interesting ideas Philips India had was this concept of shadowing to understand more about the job you want to do. Participants identify an aspirational role (or roles) based on their career plans and coaching inputs, and then get an opportunity to shadow the current role-holder for a couple of days. During this period, the 'shadowee' understands the demands of the role and the capabilities critical for success in that role. This helps provide an opportunity to observe and learn about key capabilities and skills required for an aspirational role, and also work on developing it in a more concrete way.

Nitin Paranjpe, COO of Unilever PLC, recounts these examples of coaching nudges that he received from leaders which helped him grow as a leader:

> I had once a sent a proposal to Harish Manwani, who was then the marketing controller of HUL. I didn't

get a response for a few days and I was wondering what could be the issue. The next day I met him in the hallway and asked him about the proposal. He stopped for a bit and said, 'It is short of your usually high standards.' That shook me up. While he acknowledged my standards, he also clearly gave a message that this proposal was not up to it. That moment I decided that I wanted to be known as the person who will always deliver the best that I possibly can. That was a big 'aha' moment for me.

On another occasion, **Vindi Banga**, who was my boss and went on to become chairman of HUL, and I were chatting. He then made a casual remark, not particularly to me, but generally reflecting, 'Intelligence is a great quality. But when intelligence combines with humility, that is unbeatable.' Later on, as I thought about it and looked at all the people around me, his remark hit a sweet spot, and has stayed with me ever since as one of my own principles. So you can see the big impact even a subtle advice or feedback can have on people.

- **Multidirectional career moves:** The traditional thinking was that a robust, longer term development necessitates that you move across different jobs, maybe across different product categories or geographies, and sometimes across different functions. But that kind of highly structured career path is disappearing in many organizations in the light of various changes we talked about earlier, like shorter tenures within organizations, half-life of career tracks coming down, changing business needs, personal priorities and abundance of opportunities.

For the best people, careers are now being moulded around the individual. We now need a more fluid framework, which is customized to each person. The best organizations do it in two ways. The first is by articulating appropriate career path options, more so for the first few years. Beyond that, career moves need personalization. HUL, for instance, follows a very clear principle of getting people to move between sales and marketing early on. Airtel also follows a principle of getting people to work between the circles and the central marketing teams, thus ensuring people get well-rounded experience, and the company benefits from utilizing the best talent in all areas.

Within a function, say HR, you may have a guideline of moving people from HR operations to business partnering and to an expertise area in the first five to seven years. Clarifying these principles and outlining the best profile for key roles in an organization helps people plan their careers. Secondly, we need to enable people to make relevant choices for themselves, and decide those switches or moves through a transparent open job posting system by good career counselling and career development support. There is a movement from a 'career template' approach to a 'customized to the individual' approach as we move up the hierarchy.

In the past, companies had a very 'top down' way of developing managers. In HUL, we had the functional resource committees which would identify who was capable. That unidirectional way may not work in all contexts. It may still be possible in smaller organizations where visibility of talent is high. But in large organizations, we need to create systems and platforms to enable each individual to personalize their own career growth path. We need to allow people to explore career options with curiosity and purpose. There are various essential elements that enable people to find the right roles for them, such as articulating various career path options, establishing career counselling and mentoring, setting up a system of internal job posting/internal mobility, arranging mechanisms that enable people to calibrate themselves and offering career development support.

- **From 70-20-10 to 50-30-20:** In my experience, training programmes were something everyone used to like, but we are seeing less of it. The gurus tell us that 70 per cent development is done on the job, 20 per cent through mentoring/coaching and about 10 per cent through training programmes. But paradoxically, individuals perceive development differently. Well-designed learning journeys are quite coveted, especially if they offer access to world-class faculty, concepts and facilities. And there is a strong hidden benefit—they help create strong bonds amongst the cohort of learners and inculcate a sense of pride.

  I would look at this more as 50-30-20. Especially as we are all going through so much change, there is a need for people to learn a lot from external sources: a lot of self-paced, self-directed learning, reading, structured learning journeys. But to increase their effectiveness, we need to blend learning programmes with some group projects where they work together to think through some issues in the organization. So, despite what gurus say about the effectiveness of learning programmes, I think they would play a significant role in development, given that all of us have to learn many new ideas, skills, technologies and practices in this fast changing world. The key is to design them well and provide people an opportunity to test those concepts at work. A good practice I have observed in a few companies is that they have identified learning pathways or journeys for key roles. For instance, if you aim to be a sales head or a country head, you would know what kind of learning you need to work on.

Table 4
Changing Models of Individual Development

Type of Learning	Current Model	For the Future
Learning on the job: assignments/projects	70	50
Learning from others: Coaching/mentoring /Communities of practice	20	30
Structured learning programmes	10	20

Well, we started with looking at a few principles of people

development, and then we looked at three key questions:

1. What is right talent?
2. How do we identify them?
3. How do we develop them?

It is relevant to bear in mind what **R.R. Nair**, board member and leadership coach, former HR leader, Unilever group companies, said with regard to the role of development in effective leadership:

> Effectiveness of a leader is a function of their 'technical expertise' and their 'acceptance'. That acceptance allows you to think boldly and take risks, and leaders need to invest in that. From my experience, I have seen that senior leaders sometimes have a perception of people based on their earlier experience with them. This trait can come in the way of their growth, and therefore, it is important to think of 'perception re-engineering'. Leaders have to be flexible and look for new data points and examples. HR has to play a role in getting these different perspectives and data on the table. Look at quantitative indicators, if measurable, and qualitative indicators, if verifiable. Leadership development is all about early coaching and providing crucible experiences to your future leaders which helps in annealing and hardening new capabilities.

The next question is how do we retain them? If we don't have a conscious plan for retention, then it is all wasted effort, isn't it? Having spoken with many leaders across many organizations, the biggest factor that makes a high potential leader look out for other opportunities is uncertainty. When they are not sure on their career growth within the company or their overall future in the company, they get nervy. They may be expecting a bigger role or a promotion, and if they know it is not going to happen or there are doubts around it, they start looking out. Any organization change or reshuffle at the top also creates a little bit of uncertainty. Those are times when key leaders are vulnerable.

The other reason is compensation. I don't think compensation alone is a reason for people to look out for other jobs. They will only look out if they feel that they have been unfairly dealt with or in their opinion seriously short-changed compared to their peers. What compensation does, especially when well-structured, is create some exit barriers and put up some logistical issues that make people think twice.

Well then, what have I seen working when we have to retain people? First, regular conversations with your key talent, not only by the immediate manager, but by the business head or the CEO. Be transparent about what you expect from them, listen to their personal circumstances, allay their apprehensions, but always be transparent and honest. Develop a customized career path for them, to suit their circumstances. A regular cadence of these discussions help but in times of change or in uncertain times, we need to step this up. The advantages that global multinationals have are that they have many options to provide their key talent, which may be a constraint in a smaller organization. But people appreciate honest intent, and will go with you. Hence transparent and honest career conversations, backed by right intent and efforts, always help retain people.

Compensation is an important lever too. For your high

potential leaders that you see filling up key succession roles, you might like to consider compensation at above the median. Some companies have a practice of benchmarking the high potential future successors at over seventieth percentile of the market for that job. But the key here is to lock them in with stock options. What I have seen working in large corporations is that at least 20–30 per cent of their total rewards should be through RSUs (restricted shares) which are shares granted at face value. Most companies link the amount of the annual grant to the individual's performance, and the vesting is normally over three or four years, linked to company performance. This rewards individual performance, and keeps the focus on company performance. Stock options, which are granted at market price, are more common among companies which are in early growth phase or due to go to an IPO (they create a shadow pricing system). Without getting too mired in the details, it is a good strategy to ring-fence your best leaders through a good stock plan which is market linked.

Startups use wealth creation opportunities to attract talent, drive great performance and retain talent. Oyo, for instance, provides disproportionate recognition for people who create disproportionate impact. Equity forms a large part of their rewards, while cash compensation is way below the market. For those 'high impact stars', the equity part could be disproportionately higher, even sometimes higher than their managers! The opportunity to build a new business, coupled with the opportunity for wealth creation, is what attracts great talent.

While we covered the basic principles and some practices that you could adopt, my final insight is that you may put all the best talent management practices in your organization, but if you leaders don't live it, it is of no use. The one difference between leadership development and many of the other people processes is that this is for the future. It won't impact your performance or your bonus or your team's performance that year. That's why leaders do not tend to treat it as a priority. But this will have a big impact on the future of the company, your future leadership bench and your future strategy.

And the only way to get people to take this seriously is for you, the leader, to take this seriously and set an example. You need to hold your leaders accountable for how they are developing other leaders. One way is to recognize those who develop leaders and, without hoarding them, send them to the rest of the organization. One of the ideas we tried at Airtel was to award the geography unit that did the best for talent development, especially at developing leaders who they made available for others. A small point, but it raises awareness and signals seriousness.

This is the most strategic intervention for securing the future of the company. You don't believe it? Every organization that continuously reinvented itself successfully, had done so because it had the kind of leaders needed for the future. Just look at your organization or business—what kind of leaders do you need in the future? Of course, more diverse than what you have now. What could be some of the changes in your business in the next five years, and what kind of skills or capabilities would you need in your leaders? It will definitely be different from now, and unless you build those now, your chances of success would be limited. Yes, this is seriously the most strategic thing you could do—build the right leaders for tomorrow!

Let's look at the post pandemic world. Surely you will

see a more digitized world, more connected with technology, yet working more geographically and physically distributed, with lots of fast-paced change. The leaders who would do well in the future are those who:

1. Can thrive in ambiguity, with a growth mindset
2. Lead by inspiring and building trust
3. Collaborate well with an extended eco-system
4. Are curious, agile learners who are able to see patterns

Ensuring your future leaders have these capabilities will be your key task now.

Ranjay Radhakrishnan, CHRO of Reckitt Benckiser Group PLC (RB), thinks we should make the following five vital shifts in how we develop our leaders, as we embrace a multigenerational, contemporary workforce:

1. In a world where dual careers are now the norm, career development has to shift from being predominantly 'unidirectionally set' to also being 'multidirectionally set'.
2. A move from standard career paths to mass personalization. I call it 'equifinality'—there are many ways to get to where you want to get to.
3. Shift from jobs to experiences.
4. Leadership development, which was geared towards upward hierarchical progression, is being geared towards purpose-led destinations.
5. There has to be a better balance in assessment and acceleration of high potentials, with broad-based inclusive development for all.

Key Takeaways

There are some principles that we need to keep in mind as we look at leadership development:

- People change over time, be open.
- Context and circumstances play a big role, more than we imagine.
- Everyone has their superpower and strengths, and their own sweet spot, harness it.
- Don't 'hard-code' labels on people.
- Life scars tell a story. What they have been through and their motives and values are important.

What is the right talent? This framework helps you find the right talent. It is:

(Skills, Behaviours, Experiences, Mindset) relevant for the context + strength of internal/external networks as appropriate for the role.

- To identify talent for the future, use a variety of inputs to identify the strengths of people and their likely development paths. Be wary of labelling people as high potential, but it's good to get a broad idea of top 15–20 per cent of your talent pool so you can plan development.
- Developing talent: I think the model will change from the 70 (on the job), 20 (learning from others), 10 (structured learning programmes) to 50-30-20. While on the job assignments and stretch projects are important, in the fast changing world, people have to learn from a broader ecosystem.
- A strong mix of coaching and mentoring, and having coaches who know the context helps. Develop more

internal leaders who can adopt a coaching style.

- Provide a framework for a more fluid, personalized, multidirectional career path. The destination could be the same, but people could take different routes.
- Retaining talent is critical, both through a clarity of their future growth and communication as well as through strong stock-based compensation that drives retention.
- In the end, we have to develop leaders for a very different tomorrow. This could be the most strategic action we are doing—developing future fit leaders!

References

1. Boris Groysberg, *Chasing Stars: The Myth of Talent and the Portability of Performance*, Princeton University Press, 2010.
2. Sir John Whitmore, *Coaching for Performance*, Nicholas Brealey Publishing, 2017.
3. Herminia Ibarra and Anne Scoular, 'The Leader as a Coach', *Harvard Business Review*, 2019, https://hbr.org/2019/11/the-leader-as-coach?utm_campaign=hbr&utm_source=twitter&utm_medium=social. Accessed on 7 September 2021.

10

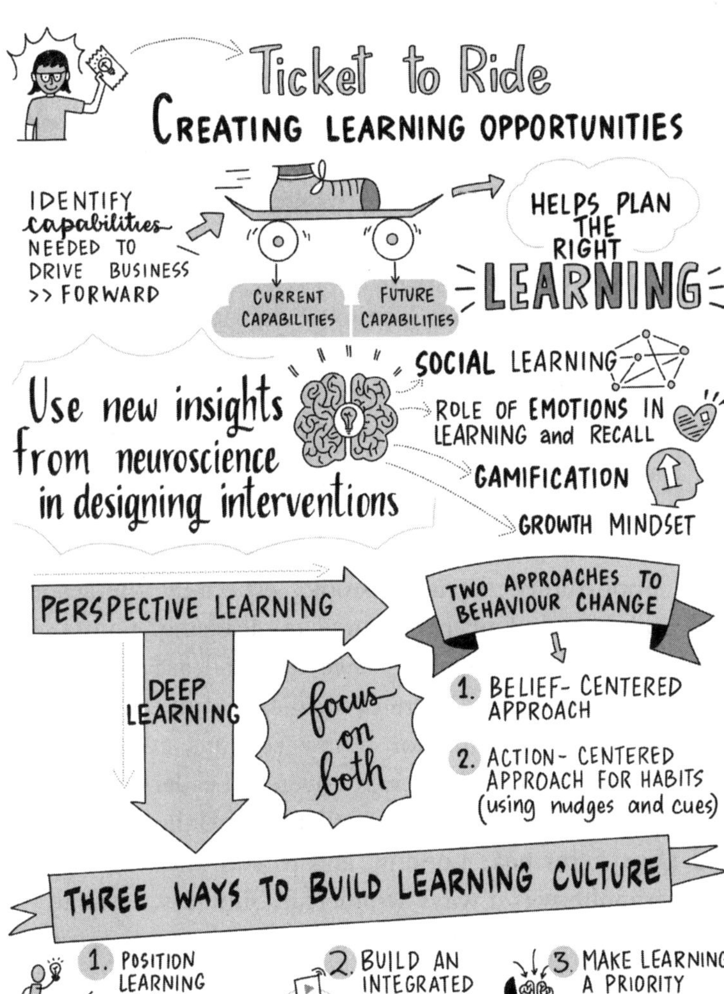

Ticket to Ride
CREATING LEARNING OPPORTUNITIES
IDENTIFY capabilities NEEDED TO DRIVE BUSINESS >> FORWARD
CURRENT CAPABILITIES
FUTURE CAPABILITIES
HELPS PLAN THE RIGHT LEARNING
Use new insights from neuroscience in designing interventions
SOCIAL LEARNING
ROLE OF EMOTIONS IN LEARNING and RECALL
GAMIFICATION
GROWTH MINDSET
PERSPECTIVE LEARNING
DEEP LEARNING
focus on both
TWO APPROACHES TO BEHAVIOUR CHANGE
1. BELIEF-CENTERED APPROACH
2. ACTION-CENTERED APPROACH FOR HABITS (using nudges and cues)
THREE WAYS TO BUILD LEARNING CULTURE
1. POSITION LEARNING AS A PART OF CAREER DEVELOPMENT
2. BUILD AN INTEGRATED LEARNING ECOSYSTEM USING TECH and ANALYTICS
3. MAKE LEARNING A PRIORITY FOR LEADERS TO ROLE MODEL

Upskilling, reskilling—these are words that you hear a lot every day, especially if you are in a technology services company. With the half-life of tech skills reducing, this is becoming the go-to mantra for all organizations. Every forum or leader talks about the need for continuous learning in organizations, but what you find is a dearth of information on how we can do this. So, this is a key outcome to focus on: How to get your employees to continuously learn and grow.

One of the jobs that I enjoyed during my career, back in 1996–97, was that of a training manager for HUL. We had a wonderful training centre called 'Gulita' on the Worli Sea Face in Mumbai, and I used to work out of there. We ran training programmes there, primarily led by our own leaders, but supplemented by a couple of external faculty, most of them professors from the IIMs. This gave me a great opportunity to meet people, especially the leaders, and understand their perspective on learning. Gulita was seen as a centre of learning—we had at least a couple of directors take sessions there every month and the chairman of HUL used to come for a few sessions every quarter. Attending a Gulita course was coveted. Leaders took pride in teaching and talking to participants. Unilever similarly had Four Acres near London, and to stay there and attend a programme was always wonderful. Similarly, GE had the famed Crotonville. Those were the heydays of corporate training centres.

While Gulita made a big impact in developing leaders and helping managers access leaders, the question was whether it could help build new capabilities across the organization. Let's look at a couple of examples of how this was done. In the mid-'90s, HUL decided to introduce TPM (Total

Productive Maintenance), a systematic and proactive way of manufacturing excellence, based on Japanese principles. This called for extensive training, with an overhaul of mindsets and habits across the factories. This was hugely successful—mainly due to the single-minded focus of the leadership on driving TPM, which ensured comprehensive training, pilots, recognizing successes, etc. Similarly, when Philips wanted to drive its transformation, it made sure that its focus on Lean was all across the organization, with every employee being trained on Lean principles, supported by a cultural transformation for all the leaders. Lean methodology is a systematic way to identify and eliminate waste, originally derived from lean manufacturing but now can be applied across any value chain. Similarly, when GE embarked on the Six Sigma initiative, there was a single-minded focus on training everyone, supported by leadership commitment to make that a key priority.

So what do we learn from this? What should we do to get every employee in the organization to learn and grow? Let's go through the few ideas here and you may have your answer.

It is one thing to say everyone should be learning something relevant and create an environment for learning. It is another thing to be more focused and think about what capabilities are needed to drive the business forward. To ensure that learning is directed both for the benefit of the organization and the individual, it is critical to articulate what capabilities will be relevant in the future.

Here is a useful framework that you could work with. It helps think about capabilities from an organization's as well as an individual's perspective.

	For Now	For the Future
Organization-led	What capabilities are relevant for the Organization Today?	What capabilities are important for the Organization in the Future?
Individual-led	What capabilities are relevant for the Individual Today?	What capabilities are important for the Individual in the Future?

This framework looks at, on the horizontal axis, the capabilities we need today, and those we need in the future. On the vertical axis, it looks at capabilities that are needed at an organizational level, for now and the future. It is important to distinguish between the individual capability and the organizational capability. In my earlier example, TPM was a capability built at the organizational level. Similarly, the quality excellence focus through Six Sigma, adopted by GE, is an organizational capability. The individual capabilities are more skills and behaviours needed for their roles. Let's take a moment to understand this with a small example.

Let's take the example of a healthcare systems organization, one that makes high-value healthcare equipment. At the organization level, it needs to build more digital services in the future. So, digital capabilities and software development are going to be key. However, currently it is focused on streamlining operations, cutting cost and coming up with more low cost products, so key capabilities needed are in Lean manufacturing. We have to be sharp on this as it is focused investment. Once you understand the capabilities needed at an organization level, you need to ensure that every employee is provided an opportunity to build those. Some of this needs to be driven strongly as a 'must have' learning for everyone. This becomes even more critical as organizations are transforming themselves for the future.

The individual capabilities are best looked at from an individual lens. Let each person look at his current role and say, 'What do I need to learn to be even better at what I am doing?' Then they should look at the future roles or aspired career and identify what else they need to develop for the future. These would normally be leadership behaviours or specific skills they can be good at. For those aspiring to be leaders, the learning is normally done across three dimensions: leading self (their own self-awareness and the inner journey), leading others (inspiring, developing and executing through the team) and leading business (understanding trends, sharpening strategy and building the ecosystem). An aggregation of these helps put together the individual level learning needed. A summary of such analysis could look like this.

	Now	In the future
Organization-led	Lean principles	Digital at scale
Individual-led	Core functional skills A menu of behavioural skills	Key leadership competencies for high potentials Specific digital technology skills

This strategic overview is needed to ensure that we are clear that the learning is focused on building the organization, as well as enabling each employee do their best in the current role and to be ready for the future. In addition, it gets the senior leadership's attention on learning, which is crucial to making this a priority. In my experience, time spent on getting this right is time truly well spent.

What Are the Choices I Need to Make in Learning Design?

We have seen earlier that while a lot of learning still happens on the job, I think it is changing from the current model of 70-20-10 to 50-30-20 (see Table 4 on Changing Models of Individual Development).

That is because of the amount of change that is there in the environment, and our need to be ahead of the change. To leapfrog and stay ahead of the curve, we need to learn new skills and also build a wider network which will enable us to stay relevant. Therefore, structured learning programmes as well as learning from others become more important. Let us look at how we can design these learning experiences.

We have immense choices in the design and delivery of learning, and I don't want to boggle you with that. But learning is one area where there have been tons of new research, especially some new insights from neuroscience. You could start with understanding the SCARF model developed by David Rock where he talks of five domains: status, certainty, autonomy, relatedness and fairness which activate the same threat and reward responses in the brain that we rely on for survival.[1] The more I read about the newer research insights on this, the more fascinated I become about this. Let me try and articulate the insights that are critical to your idea of a good learning design:

1. Our brain is constantly adapting to the environment. This is called 'neuroplasticity'. At any age, as we experience and learn, groups of neurons fire up new pathways and connections. Our brains are physically shaped by our experiences. So learning is continuous, and we need to design the right experiences at all times, not just when a person is doing a learning programme. Carol Dweck's research on 'growth mindset' proves that efforts can increase capabilities and that capabilities are not fixed.[2] Moreover, research has shown that if we first think about how we are going to learn a particular skill or a topic, we tend to learn better.
2. Learning socially is more natural to us than learning alone. A couple of concepts will help us here. We have 'mirror neurons'. These neurons fire when you watch the actions of others. Second, our brains are not good at considering different points of view by ourselves; when we interact socially with others, we tend to empathize and critically consider different points of view helping us to learn. The brain's primary environment is the web of social relationships which helps stimulate neuroplasticity, positive emotions and learning. Using learning cohorts, group learning activities and other peer learning nudges are critical.
3. Emotions play a big role in learning. Research has shown that the same area of the brain deals with emotions and memories—the prefrontal cortex. Positive emotions help in learning, whereas fear and anxiety impede learning. Research has also shown

that where learning is made more personal, it makes a big difference. Bring positive emotions and a personal context to learning. Getting people to relate the learning to their personal circumstances and linking it with their personal aspirations for change really help.[3]

4. Gamification helps as it triggers release of dopamine (the 'feel good' hormone when you are rewarded), serotonin (the mood hormone) and endorphins (due to thrill and excitement), that create positive emotions and help in learning. Gamified learning also helps recall as the part of the brain that is associated with knowledge recall, the hippocampus, is also activated by some game play. But gamification is not the answer to every learning. It builds an interest in exploring and continuing with the learning and a quick recall, but needs to be supported by other means to build deep skills. But, the key principle is to make learning fun.
5. We can broadly divide learning into two parts, both of which are important, and depicted in a T shape. The first is 'perspective' learning or broadening your perspective and understanding. This is critical to help you connect the dots, look at the big picture and think strategically. This is the horizontal line in the T. We also need to be able to do something very well. It could be a behavioural skill or a technical skill. This is 'deep' learning, the vertical line in the T. Obviously, each of these is developed differently and we need to keep that in mind. To master a behaviour or a skill, you need to practice it, get feedback and do 'hands-on' work on it. Some kind of gamified

assessment or a hackathon is a way to ensure that the skills have been internalized.

6. When we deal with leadership behaviours, my experience is that we need to use two ways of enabling change: the 'belief-centred' and the 'action-centred approaches. The belief-centred approach draws on the work of Argyris and Schon on double loop learning that involves teaching people to think more deeply about their own assumptions and beliefs.[4 5] Take an example of persons who are poor delegators or try to over-supervise. Through a dialogue, let's try and get them to understand their beliefs and assumptions and get them to rethink those. May be it's to do with their assumptions of competence of others, and you try and work on that. The action-centred way is an outside-in approach. You ask them to look at their actions and habits, and get them to do those differently. In the case of a poor delegator, you could ask him/her to clarify the work delegated and review it only once a week. My learning has been that working on actions, one step at a time, helps bring an overall change, focus on making one change consciously, embed it and move to the next action. However, as you can see, this kind of behavioural change cannot be done by just a learning programme, it needs individual coaching. Some of the new research on habits has given us more insights on how we can use triggers and cues to get people to exhibit new behaviours.[6] Another way to reinforce this is to use 'nudge technology'—using technology and the right analytics, we ensure the right behavioural nudges are given to people

at right times, thus prompting behaviour change through micro feedback and actions.

These are the basic principles that are important to keep in mind when we think of designing any kind of learning. We have to make choices from among these to design the right learning based on the need as well as the group of employees. One key truth: the biggest vehicle for our learning and development is the job that each of us is doing. That is the stage, that is the laboratory where each one develops. Learning programmes help, but needs to be taken back and applied in the context of our everyday work. But, I see these becoming more important in the fast changing future world. We may go back to the days of large 'corporate universities' but albeit in a very virtual way.

We now accept the fact that learning is a lifelong process, and the key is to teach people how to learn. Which brings us to our key challenge- 'how do we institutionalize learning'?

The best companies do a fabulous job of institutionalizing learning and that is at the heart of their success. My own experience, having looked at various different organizations from technology to FMCG, is that there are three core ways through which we can institutionalize learning:

1. **Position learning as integral to career development:** People will take up learning if they see it is closely linked to their own development. Our annual performance development conversations with employees should result in a clear and simple learning plan. There are organizations that track development goals as seriously as business goals. For instance, 3M gets people to put down their development goals and track them as part of the performance development conversations. Our

career architecture and career paths should clarify what skills and capabilities are important in each role so people work on them. In technology companies, creating a skills architecture and gamifying progress is essential. Having a safe and transparent system where people can get their skills and behaviours assessed, like a development centre, helps focus on their learning plan. In the past, the traditional learning-oriented companies like GE and Unilever would have a certain signature learning programme linked to career progression. While those programmes are seen as elitist, one way that really works is to articulate powerful learning journeys and having a transparent mechanism for people to get enrolled on such a journey.

2. **Enable with intuitive learning architecture and eco-systems:** Leading on from our first section on identifying the right focus of learning, we need to provide a menu of learning options, both organization directed, as well as individual directed learning programmes. It is important to remove all friction to learning, make learning accessible anytime, and ensure all our learning programmes are built on the six principles articulated earlier. Small rewards for learning are critical; they help build the habit. Of course, having an intuitive learning system, where people can learn on their own, really helps. At the heart of this is good quality analytics. The richness of data from performance to all elements of learning is critical to develop right nudges and reinforcement. At Infosys, one of the things that really helped us was the versatility of Lex, our learning system (Wingspan is the external brand name). It enables learning across laptops and mobiles 24/7, with

gamified social learning features, proctored assessments and telemetry and analytics that does a great job of keeping learners on track. Technology is a key enabler of learning these days.

You have to create a buzz around learning and make people feel they have made a true investment in themselves. We have to create the full eco-system of mentors, of teachers, of learning projects, a learning plan linked to the role and performance expected, all linked to where the organization needs to build capability.

Let's look at the example of Titan that created the concept of Learning Circles. Key staff and store managers were trained as trainers and their role extended to training other staff in their region. This enabled them to rapidly multiply the capability to train in the workplace and in store, and helped in faster roll out of new initiatives. Using the Kaizen approach for continuous improvement also helps to institutionalize training at the frontline level, both in sales and in manufacturing. Philips has a global Kaizen competition with teams selected at each country level. Titan also does a national Kaizen mela.

3. **Make learning a key priority and hold leaders accountable for it:** The key is to leverage your leaders and encourage them to teach. This also builds empathy and collegiality and creates a culture of sharing, learning and growing together. It is important to develop relevant simple metrics that focus on the capability development in each unit. It might be more easy in tech companies where you could talk of the number of people skilled and certified, etc., but I think each industry can adopt some metrics of capability development. Also, track the

time leaders are spending in learning, in teaching and in sharing.

Whichever capability you want to build, it is important you institutionalize it because learning is not a one-off event. And any one of the above three approaches won't be enough. You may need a confluence of all three levers to make a long-term difference. Take the following example offered by **Manoj Garg,** CHRO, Dr Lal Pathlabs Limited:

> Dr Lal Pathlabs is engaged in the business of healthcare service delivery, with more than 200 labs and around 3,500 sample collection outlets. The customer facing frontline employees are distributed across the company. Healthcare being a very service-oriented category, we needed to train all our customer facing employees on various customer handling topics as well as provide regular refresher trainings. Classroom sessions were not an option. So we decided to roll out a programme under which we selected 150 employees from the frontline roles (selected from the local geographical area) and trained them as trainers for the customer service programmes. These people were then given the task to travel within their local area and train staff. The top 10 trainers among the group are felicitated annually with Dronacharya award in our annual award function. These 150 employees have been able to give us a coverage of training more than 5,000 employees, at least two to three times a year. They have developed training, presentation skills and a cult level status within their peer group.
>
> The best part is that we have been able to sustain this initiative over the last four years, and even during

the pandemic, the trainers have used digital medium like Teams to continue the training journey.

Build a Learning Culture

In the end, nothing works sustainably in an organization unless it is a deeply embedded habit, a set of behaviours that are repeatedly done by each one of us. There are many companies where there is a strong culture of learning—Infosys, IBM, HUL, Wipro, TVS and others. What is behind that culture? It starts with leaders and their commitment and focus on learning and building capabilities for the future. They give time to learning. They clearly link capabilities to the future success of the business and put in place plans to build those capabilities. They walk the talk. They look at failures and success as learning opportunities. They are the role-models. Enable your people to network with leaders and learn from them, with a constant focus on learning from experience. Reflect on what went well and what didn't go as planned.

In addition to the leadership focus, these companies integrate learning with all aspects of their people processes—to the strategy, to performance development, to career growth, to job rotations and to recognition and rewards. That integrated ecosystem will create a winner.

Here is another example by **B.P. Biddappa**, global HR head for Home Care, Unilever, and former HR director of Hindustan Unilever Ltd:

> A learning culture happens with the confluence of three drivers—a need for institutional capabilities that could get the business competitive advantage, a leadership that believes in continuous learning and meritocracy

and a hunger in people to personally grow and develop themselves as professionals creating bigger and bigger impact. A secret sauce that helps this happen is putting people in different roles, cultures or business contexts so they keep learning and relearning.

Krishnakumar Natarajan, co-founder and managing partner, Mela Ventures, who also co-founded Mindtree, has this to say on creating a learning culture:

Continuous learning is critical in the New World for individual and professional success. Individuals need to reignite their 'childlike' curiosity and use every opportunity to enhance their capabilities. Organizations should create an enabling environment but the responsibility for learning outcomes must lie with individuals.

At Mindtree, we created a new approach of 'experiential' learning where people learnt through doing, devoid of any assessment mechanism. Learning through cohorts was encouraged and physical/digital infrastructure to support 24x7 interactions of the cohorts was enabled. Effective storytelling and walking the talk by leadership enables a learning culture. Leaders drive a learning culture and a learning culture enables an organization to sustain and thrive.

◆

Milind Pant, CEO of Amway, along with the company's global leadership team, helped its more than 15,000 employees across the world recapture the mindset of its founders on its journey to transform from a traditional direct selling company into an entrepreneur-led, health and wellness company designed for anyone with a passion, a positive attitude and a mobile phone.

Lifelong Learning—It's the Journey and the Destination

One of my personal leadership mantras is, 'be a lifelong learner'. I grew up in the lower-tier cities across India, in the foothills of the Himalayas. My childhood, while full of love, was one with modest material means. We never had a television until my early teens, and an air conditioner at home was out of the question. However, I always felt rich, with a strong foundation of 'sanskar' from my parents. This is the north star of family values, hard work and a love for continuous learning.

In my early teens, my father encouraged me to listen to BBC radio and read newspapers. This was to build my perspective and improve my English. I am quite sure I did neither to his satisfaction! However, it triggered a quest for lifelong learning that I am forever grateful for—one that many individuals across the world share and that organizations can foster.

Fast forward to my first job after earning my Master's in International Business. I was expecting a thrilling assignment with my new employer, Unilever, as a manager in their international key accounts team—perhaps involving travel to New York or London for meetings with high-profile customers. Instead, I found myself sitting in humid, 110-degree heat, helping sort moist, semi-processed leather inside a tannery in India's Tamil Nadu province. That foul smell is still in my nostrils almost three decades later!

This felt, in many ways, like the opposite of career growth, but it turns out it was exactly where I needed to be. I was growing as a person and as a professional, even if I didn't know it yet.

The phrase 'growth mindset' is well-known these days and I'm a big believer in its principles. At the core, it is about being uncomfortable with the status quo, being bold and unafraid to fail, and being a continuous learner. As defined by Dr Carol Dweck, it involves seeing challenges as opportunities to learn and advance, and accepting setbacks as a foundational part of growth.

But learning to see life through this lens takes time and practice. Put simply, one doesn't naturally think, 'Today, I will celebrate failure.' It took me a long time, and many roles, each full of unique lessons—some harder than others—to get there. And at organizations with long legacies of success, such as Amway's of more than 60 years, it can feel strange at first.

Amway's co-founders, Rich DeVos and Jay Van Andel, lived the growth mindset. They challenged the status quo, woke each day with a sense of adventure, lived to serve millions of entrepreneurs known as Amway business owners around the world and led with their hearts.

As we began embarking on a multi-year company transformation that would require employees to be agile, our global leadership team and I started by asking ourselves what Rich and Jay might do. We decided to start with the simple step of sharing—broadcasting even—our own growth mindset experiences, especially those involving failure. We wanted to create an environment in which discussing lessons learned from failures was as important as sharing results. We encouraged leaders to focus conversations on how employees showed their 'love to learn' mindset over specific project or programme metrics.

This effort remains a work in progress. We're helping each other realize that growth will happen often when we least expect it. While it can be exhilarating and fulfilling, it doesn't always feel that way at first. In fact, it's often uncomfortable. But that discomfort is a leading indicator that one is truly learning and growing. Along the way, it is helping us tackle an evolving global e-commerce and social platform landscape and helping our entrepreneurs succeed in building communities around their health and wellness passions.

This journey of learning and growth is, in many ways, its own reward. It is inspiring in all of the best ways. Today, I see a spirit of adventure and optimism in so many of my colleagues and the entrepreneurs we support. Together, we are approaching every speedbump, every unprecedented event (like the COVID-19 pandemic) with a resilience and passion that proves growth isn't just a mindset, it's a lifestyle—and a very rewarding one at that.

Key Takeaways

- To start with, be more focused and think about what capabilities are needed to drive the business forward. Articulate what capabilities will be relevant in the future and also look at capabilities that each individual should have for today and in the future. This perspective of the individual's and the organization's capabilities helps plan the right learning.
- Use some of the newer insights from neuroscience research in designing learning interventions. Social learning, role of emotions in learning and recall, gamification as well as promoting a growth mindset are key principles to leverage
- There is perspective learning and there is deep learning, the horizontal and the vertical of the T shape skills needed. We learn each of these differently.
- When we look at behaviour change, we can adopt two approaches—the belief-centred approach or the action-centred approach. A lot of newer research on habits has given us insights on how to use the action-centred approach better with nudges and cues.
- The key is to institutionalize learning in an organization and create a learning culture. Three key ways we can do that are:
  a. Position learning as integral to career development, clarifying which skills and

behaviours would be needed in different roles and providing opportunities to learn.

b. Build an integrated learning ecosystem using technology and analytics. Technology is increasingly becoming core to learning, with algorithms providing insights and nudges, a learning system that enables anywhere-anytime learning, and creating a buzz around learning.
c. Make this a priority for leaders. Leverage them. Let them be role models, visibly leading the way.

References

1. Dr David Rock and Dr Al Ringleb, *Handbook of NeuroLeadership*, Amazon Digital Services, 2013.
2. Carol S. Dweck, *Mindset*, Random House, 2006.
3. Chai M. Tyng, Hafeez U. Amin, Mohamad N. M. Saad and Aamir S. Malik, 'The Influences of Emotions on Memory and Learning', NCBI, 24 August 2017, https://www.ncbi.nlm.nih.gov/pmc/articles/PMC5573739/. Accessed on 20 October 2021.
4. Chris Argyris, *Knowledge for Action: A Guide to Overcoming Barriers to Organizational Change*. Jossey-Bass Publishers, 1993.
5. Chris Argyris and Donald A. Schon, *Organizational Learning: A Theory of Action Perspective*. Addison-Wesley Publishing Co., 1978.
6. James Clear, *Atomic Habits: An Easy and Proven Way to Build Good Habits and Break Bad Ones*, Random House, 2018.

11

Come Together

GETTING YOUR WORKFORCE AT THEIR BEST

WE STILL TAKE A VERY 'COGNITIVE APPROACH' TO ENGAGEMENT.
WE NEED AN 'EMOTION-BASED APPROACH' TOO.

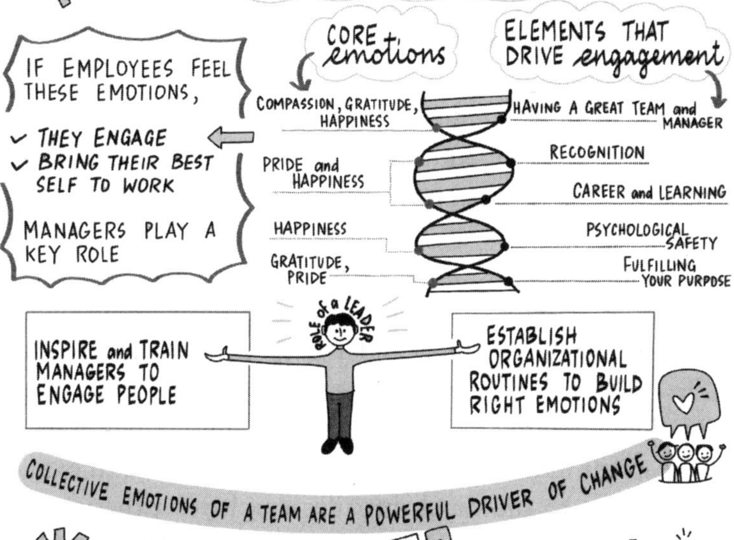

INSIGHTS FROM LATEST RESEARCH on HAPPINESS

YOU CAN BUILD HAPPINESS BY INTENTIONAL ACTIVITIES OF GRATITUDE, KINDNESS, COMPASSION, MINDFULNESS

TO ENGAGE IN VIRTUAL WORLD, MANAGERS NEED TO:
- FOCUS ON EMPATHY
- BE RESPONSIVE
- PROVIDE CLARITY
- BUILD TRUST

HAVE REAL TIME MEASURES OF ENGAGEMENT WITH MANAGERS USING TECHNOLOGY

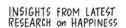

EMPLOYEE PERCEPTION + ANALYTICS FROM EMPLOYEE TOUCHPOINTS

The word 'engagement' is something I have started hearing more of in the last 10–12 years. We didn't have much of a hype on engagement in the '90s or in the early 2000s. At Unilever, we used to do a global people survey once every two years, and most of it was pen-and-paper-based. The results used to take about three to six months and by the time we cascaded and did team discussions, it was almost a year. We did not dissect or discuss the engagement levels of various teams. Attrition was low, across all of Unilever in Asia (except China), so this was not an issue.

Cut to another industry and another company. I moved to Bharti Airtel in 2007, and the first thing Sunil Bharti Mittal told me was to make a plan to improve engagement. Attrition was high at the frontline. We had a Gallup 'engagement survey' done every year and this resulted in a flurry of activities to drive up 'engagement'. Engagement took on a new meaning and I tried to learn more about it. In the last decade, engagement has become a buzzword, with lots of different models talking of various hues of engagement. Of late, there has also been a move to expand engagement to the much broader employee experience.

Maslow's hierarchy of needs and Herzberg's two factor theory of motivators and hygiene factors made sense and gave me an idea of what motivates people.[1] We also know that managers have a big role in motivating their teams—they can make or break it. But this engagement idea was new, and I was curious to understand more about what it really meant and what drove it. I was told that engagement means 'discretionary effort by employees', and that it was driven more by 'emotional engagement'. Every consulting firm had their model of engagement—but I realized that they varied in what and how they measured, but were conceptually similar. I read Daniel Pink, and he spoke of Mastery, Autonomy and Purpose—the three truths of motivation.[2] Based on all my understanding over these years, let me try and articulate my views or rather my model of engagement. But first, we have to understand the context of our workforce and the rapidly changing business environment. We now have a workforce predominantly comprising millennials and Gen Z. Any model of engagement needs to be well-researched keeping this context in mind. Let us start with defining engagement. It builds further on the concept of motivation—it is the passion, the involvement, the motivation employees bring to their jobs and the emotional investment they make in the organizations. Engagement brings more emotions into play, more than just a cognitive appraisal of what the job or the company offers.

But the paradox is that we still approach 'engagement' with a very 'cognitive' or rational problem solving method; that has been my greatest learning, and has been at the root of wherever I have failed to build engagement. So this realization is coming from some of my failures, and further prompted by some of the new literature on emotions. Therefore, we need to first understand what drives engagement and then dig into the how of building the emotional connection.

The New Model of Engagement

There is a lot of new literature now on what drives engagement, especially amongst the current millennial workforce. With my insights into working across a few sectors and my discussions with many practitioners, my model of engagement is based on five key pillars.

Table 5
Five Core Pillars of Engagement

Pillars	Great team and manager	Recognition	Learning and career growth	Psychological safety	Sense of fulfilling a purpose
Questions we seek to answer	*Do I enjoy working with this team and manager? Do I like being with them?*	*Am I recognized appropriately? Am I rewarded fairly?*	*Is there challenge in my job? Am I learning in my job? Am I growing?*	*Do I feel psychologically safe? Am I able to be authentic and express myself? Do I have reasonable autonomy?*	*Am I making a meaningful impact? Am I able to achieve my purpose? Is the purpose of the organization appealing to me?*
Need	Social	Self-esteem	Personal growth	Being at your best	Belief and emotional commitment

At the very base of that is the yearning to meet our social needs, that's a primary need. Every employee wants to enjoy working with their team and manager. We are socially geared, so having great colleagues is the first thing that is needed for engagement. Much research, including a latest McKinsey report, confirms the predominant role of managers or bosses in employee satisfaction.[3] That is followed by the need for recognition. Recognition helps generate pride and self-esteem. Building on that is everyone's need for personal growth—some interesting challenges in the job, and the consequent learning and growth. Finally, it is about every person being at their best, and to be that, they need an environment where they feel psychological safe, and where they are able to be authentic and achieve their personal goals and aspirations.

Let us spend some time understanding psychological safety. Research shows that this is indeed a distinguishing feature of great teams. In organizations and teams that are focused on innovation, this could be the most important element that determines effectiveness. Timothy Clark lists out the four steps to psychological safety.[4] At the base is member safety or inclusion safety, where an employee feels accepted for who she or he is. The second level is learner safety, where employees feel safe to ask questions, make mistakes and learn. The next stage is contributor safety, where you feel safe to make contribution with your skills and abilities. The final stage is challenger safety where employees feel safe to speak up and question the status quo when they see an opportunity for improvement. This is a useful guide to think about where your teams are and the practices you can introduce to increase psychological safety in teams.

So, in summary, this is my framework for thinking about employee engagement: **T** (team) **R** (recognition) **L** (learning), **P** (psychological safety) and **P** (purpose). Is it any different from any other form of employee engagement? Probably yes; it is more focused on things that really make a difference on the ground and more relevant for the future, based on latest research. However, we need the right sustainable actions to deliver on these elements. But more importantly, the key is, how do we consciously understand emotions that are associated with this and work on them. That's the difference.

Before we go further, let us step back and look at how emotions are important here. We know that true engagement is when there is a greater emotional involvement. More than a rational, cognitive assessment of the above elements, which is important, we are also driven by our emotions. Our decision-making is influenced by emotions. So while we work on delivering the rational elements in the above model, we need to also simultaneously work on generating the relevant emotions. This mix of 'rational' and the 'emotional' is critical; envisage them as two strands of a DNA, each providing its unique 'hook', but working in tandem. That is the real insight we need to build on.

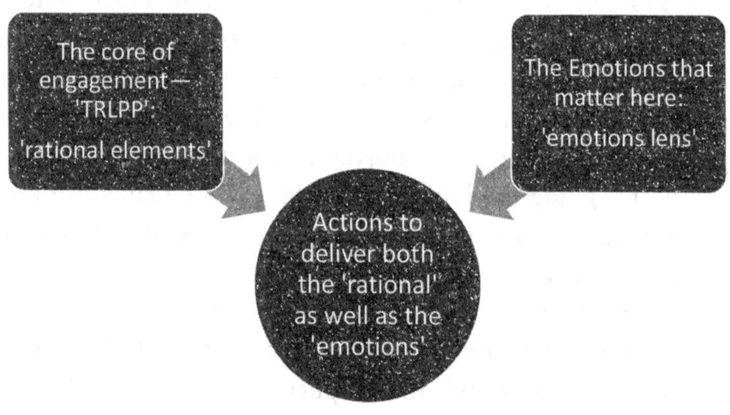

The Emotions Lens

Let's try and understand the specific emotions that are at the root of engagement along these five dimensions.

Table 6
Pillars of Engagement and Their Relevant Emotions

Key element	Concomitant emotions
Great team and manager	Compassion, gratitude, happiness
Recognition	Pride, gratitude
Learning and growth	Pride, gratitude
Psychological safety	Happiness, gratitude
Purpose, achieving goals	Gratitude, pride

As you can see there are four core emotions at the heart of engagement. Based on the work of David DeSteno,[5] Sonja Lyubomirsky,[6] Martin Seligman[7] and others, here is a quick overview of these emotions.

Compassion: It is an emotion that just goes beyond empathy and makes people want to help. They not only understand the emotions of the others, but also are moved to help. This is a crucial emotion needed to build great teams and collaboration across the company. This makes people feel included and enjoy being part of a team.

Pride: There are broadly two types of pride. Pride attributed to controllable causes is called 'authentic pride', i.e. 'I succeeded because I put in efforts,'. Then there is pride due to stable causes which is called 'hubristic pride,' i.e.,'I succeeded because of who I am.' Authentic pride is linked to various aspects of resilience, effort, pro-social and positive leadership behaviours, whereas hubristic pride leads to narcissistic behaviours and interpersonal conflicts.

Gratitude: This is a powerful emotion that makes people go the extra mile. We feel grateful if other people have invested in us and that makes us willing to return the favour in future. Gratitude also makes us take a long-term view of things, be less self-centred and collaborate with others.

Happiness: It can be defined as 'subjective well-being'. Of late, there has been significant research on happiness, and what causes it. Happiness leads to more pro-social behaviour and more commitment, and is caused by many factors. Helping others, having a sense of gratitude, following your passion and good social connections, all help us in happiness.

My insight is that the 'emotions lens' is important, and we have quite under-emphasized it compared to the rational elements. If we change our perspective to ask 'how can I ensure these emotions are present in my teams or employees?' and start planning actions or routines that bring these emotions among the team, I think we will make a big impact on engagement. So, first, this calls for a change of perspective. Think about what emotions you would like to see in your team, and plan for those. But you might ask, can I really plan for certain emotions? Yes, of course. Emotions are but our response to any event or stimulus. For instance, if you want to see emotions of gratitude, consider mentoring your team. When they see time invested in their development, that would lead to an emotion of immense gratitude. If we consciously think of creating certain emotions, it is possible and is actually much more powerful than any rational approach to motivating and engaging people.

Here comes the easy part on actions! Honestly, as you can see, a lot of the levers of good engagement is with the manager, supported of course by the organizational systems. Also, it is no rocket science. If a manager acts humanly, with the right intent and keeping her/his team's growth and well-being as the prime focus, you will have great engagement. The emotions needed are not unique; they are basic human emotions and we experience them every day. The only issue is that we don't all do the right things consciously.

So if we are to drive the right engagement, the first step is for each of the leaders to understand the basic drivers of engagement and the emotions that are needed. We need to believe this at an intuitive level, and make it the core of our people philosophy.

As we can see, the person who can make the biggest impact at all levels are the managers. If they do the right things, you have great engagement. So we need to focus on enabling them, training them, letting them experience this and making them the champions of engagement. Celebrate them. The oft maligned 'middle manager' actually plays a key role in managing emotions of the team and in building engagement. Make them conscious of the key role of people development they are playing and inspire them to be good at it. At the same time, support them with organizational practices and routines that enable them to combine the 'rational' as well as the 'emotional' part of engagement. In a way, your role as a leader is just to focus on two key priorities:

1. Inspire and train your managers to engage people by understanding emotions.
2. Establish organizational routines to build the right emotions and to enable deep engagement.

But you might ask, what kind of actions will build emotions and also deliver on the 'rational' expectations? Here are some ideas that I have seen working. This is not an exhaustive list, and only some ideas that seem to work. The key here is to design and implement actions and initiatives that deliver both the engagement drivers as well as the desired emotions.

Table 7
Linking Engagement and Emotions through Common Actions

The engagement drivers	**The core emotions**	**Actions**
Great team and manager	Compassion, gratitude, happiness	Show gratitude to others in the team regularly. Celebrate team success, but let team members thank people who helped them. Create a practice in the team of celebrating the people who go out of their way to offer help to others.
Recognition	Pride, gratitude	Build a routine of both the 'little' everyday praise and the 'big' periodic recognition. Establish a formal recognition system that managers can use. Encourage teams to have their own recognition ideas. Have more transparency in the rewards processes.

Learning and growth	Pride, gratitude	Ensure right amount of challenge is present in each job. Build a strong mentoring culture. Let managers invest personal time talking to people about their development. Establish a robust learning framework that also recognizes people learning. Create a framework for people to share their learning, through communities, as mentors, as teachers and bloggers. Establish systems for people to look for jobs internally- and reduce friction in internal mobility. Create an internal gig culture. Institutionalize a career counselling and support framework.
Psychological safety	Happiness	Promote sessions in teams where they openly give feedback to each other. Train managers to be empathetic and inclusive. Establish peer feedback and an open 360-degree feedback for development.

Purpose, achieving goals	Gratitude, pride	Encourage volunteering for causes dear to people. Create communities in the organization to drive common causes—environment, education, etc. Encourage job crafting. Create opportunities for employees to talk about what they really want to achieve and help them do that.

Leaders who communicate regularly build the right foundation for engagement. While many companies do this well, let me give you an example from Oyo Rooms. 'How do you build a sense of purpose' with employees is the core question they try and answer. The founder and CEO, Ritesh Agarwal, takes pains to connect with employees. They organize an all-employee town hall every week and a 'top 200' meeting every fortnight. In these meetings, they focus on three core objectives: reinforcing 'why do we exist' (reiterating their purpose), updating people on the business and answering any questions or concerns. Every month, they attempt to touch every single employee. This transparent communication builds the emotions of pride and optimism amongst the team.

Let me extend the concept of emotions to other specific situations. Take the various situations that many of us, as leaders, face in respect to motivating or engaging our teams. Consider, for instance, that the results of one quarter are down and you want to get the team focused on the future and go for their targets positively. What emotions are needed in your team to do this? Clearly, emotions of optimism and maybe pride. If you plan actions and initiatives that lead to optimism and pride in the team, your chances of mobilizing their commitment and meeting the targets are high. So, how do you create optimism and pride? By talking about how the target can be achieved, by creating a buzz around the initial small wins, celebrating successes, reminding them of their past success against odds, etc. Similarly, if you find that collaboration between two teams within your function is low, the key to drive this is to create emotions of gratitude and compassion in the teams. You get the drift, right? In any specific situation, look at what emotions you need to see in your teams that will lead to success, and try and build those.

We do a lot of work on change management, and often those end in a disaster. If only we did this kind of an 'emotion state' assessment more often, it might help us manage change and transformation in the business.

I am reminded of a huge transformation we did in Bharti Airtel over a decade back. We got the three consumer facing businesses together, from being separate entities. This meant that the leadership teams of each business, at various levels, were dismantled as they were forged into one integrated go-to market structure with independent marketing. We also changed the sales model of the broadband team, from company salesmen to a dealer model, leading to some redundancies. It was a big change and brought a greater strategic alignment, but with a hit on employee morale. However, given the speed with which we implemented the change, I felt that I had failed to read into the emotions of people. Even if people had an alternate role but had to move to a different business, they had strong negative emotions about it. And, that has been my learning. Working with the emotions of people, even if it takes more time, gives you more sustainable change.

In summary, what I propose is that to get the best from people, we have to tap into their emotions. We normally tend to approach things rationally and predominantly use the cognitive approaches. Leveraging emotions is not easy; it is a skill that we need to build. It is about recognizing emotions, about understanding which emotions are needed for certain behaviours and having a feel of how to build those collective emotions in the team. Moreover, to be successful in leveraging emotions, the manger must be authentic and have credibility. The collective emotions of a group of people or a team is a powerful driver for change. It is critical that managers of the future build this important muscle.

There is a lot of new literature on happiness and what makes people happy. The Bhagavad Gita was clear that attachment to material things could lead to unhappiness, and that deep self-knowledge ('brahma vidya' and 'Gnana yoga') was the way out of the unhappiness trap. Buddha also spoke of renunciation of attachments and practising mindfulness. Well, those truths are still relevant and current research validates it. Let me try and capture some of the latest insights that we could use in our work in organizations.

There is a factor called 'hedonic adaptation'—our happiness threshold quickly comes back to a certain set level even after critical life events. For instance, you get lucky with a lottery. There is a spike in happiness, but shortly afterwards you revert to your set threshold of happiness! In her research, Sonja Lyubomirsky, a professor of Psychology in the University of California and a well-known happiness researcher and author, says that the difference in happiness amongst two groups of people can be explained by this: 50 per cent of the difference is due to genetic factors (your set point), 40 per cent due to focused intentional actions and only 10 per cent due to external life circumstances (like whether you are rich or poor).[8] So the key to managing your happiness are the intentional actions. So what are some of those deliberate actions? Here they are:

1. Finding meaning in your life is important. People involved in absorbing or challenging activities that they find meaningful often enter a state of flow, where they become fully immersed in their work. Experiences tend to make us happier, more than things or possessions, because you can relive the experiences at a later point and feel happy.
2. Being kind to others and doing acts of kindness increases your own happiness, more than one might imagine. Similarly, doing something for larger good makes you happy.
3. Regular expressions of gratitude promote optimism, better health and general satisfaction with life. Giving thanks or maintaining a gratitude journal clearly impacts your happiness.
4. People who report being happier tend to have more social connections. The quality and depth of these connections matter more than the quantity.
5. Regular physical activity, as well as good rest and sleep give happiness a boost. Mindfulness, which is being attentive to your thoughts and emotions and being in the moment, helps too. Any practice that helps you avoid unhealthy social comparison leads to happiness.

So how can these insights on our happiness help organizations engage people? Clearly, this research supports my hypothesis that creating emotions of gratitude, compassion and pride in our teams is important. Designing opportunities for people to choose the intentional activities that help generate those emotions will be helpful. You can see how peer recognition or expressing gratitude becomes so important. Thanking a team member makes both the 'giver' and the 'receiver' happy.

As we look at the post-pandemic world, where many of us will work remotely more often, engagement takes on a slightly different hue. A new study on what employees look for in a good manager in this remote world is slightly different from the past. In a more virtual environment, someone emerged as a good manager based on their achievement and behaviours, whereas in a less virtual environment, their traits played a key role.[9] Therefore, in a remote environment, people don't give a premium to the charisma and confidence of managers, but they want managers who are quick to respond, are organized and facilitate connections between colleagues. We need to develop managers who are productive, disciplined in terms of running meeting and calls, who provide clarity, are empathetic and approachable and build trust.[10]

Do people prefer remote work? Many do, as it gives them flexibility and they can avoid commuting to work, as we hear from GitLab, one of the world's largest 'all-remote' company.[11] But they would also miss the camaraderie and interactions in the office. So they may feel lonely and disconnected over time. Brainstorming, creative discussions, project planning types of activities, though they can be done remotely, would benefit more from in- person face to face interaction. Therefore, engagement actions to make people feel included would be critical. The manager needs to play the role of a 'corporate evangelist' connecting others to events in the organization and being the larger face of the organization.[12] An offshoot of this remote working and loneliness could be mental health issues, so that's an area we need to focus more on. Training managers and teams on mental well-being, and helping them detect signs of mental ill-health early, would be critical in addition to a lot of proactive activities on emotional and social well-being. Many companies have the concept of mental health first-aiders who are quick to spot issues and provide first-level help. In Infosys, there is an employee volunteer group called Samaritans, who are trained in preliminary counselling and they help talk to people who need help. If the issues persist, then they are referred to expert mental health counsellors.

Engaging Blue Collar Workforce

The blue collar workforce is changing. A couple of years back, I visited GE's factory in Pune, which was doing machining of some aircraft engine components, and found that every person there was either a diploma holder or an engineer. The workforce varies tremendously by industry and region, but one thing is clear—the focus is changing from the old collectivist approach to blue collar to a more individual focus on development. I see some of the hi-tech companies leading in this. 3M has a robust performance development process through simple appraisals and individual development plan. The workforce of today is more aspirational, and engaging them on their development and growth would be important. Communication and transparency of business performance builds trust. Some of the best ways to engage blue collar is through the various participatory programmes pioneered by the Japanese: Kaizen (the business philosophy referring to continual improvement), the Toyota production system, etc. The core principles behind these successful methods are empowerment, involvement, transparent communication and a focus on continuous development, strongly linking individual development to company results.

A strong focus on family growth was very critical for this group. I remember in the Ponds factory in Pondicherry, in the years around the turn of the millennium, one of the big focus areas was to support the children of the workmen to study and do well, including support for higher education. That has resulted in a whole generation of those children now being engineers and doctors and changing their lives forever. I can go on. There are numerous examples of similar success in the industry, but all that we now need to keep in mind is that with the changing demographics and aspirations of the blue collar, we need to bring in more of the modern positive psychology principles to engage and develop them.

Lots of new advances have been made in how we track and measure how our teams feel, and how they engaged, etc. Technology has now given us various new ways to measure team satisfaction levels. From a survey once or twice a year we can move to some real-time data. Using the benefit of technology in Infosys, we created a model that polled people on just two-three questions (both on their laptops and mobile) every fortnight and it helped build real-time dashboards that managers could use to see their team's engagement. We also created three indices to measure different elements: an EVP index that measured satisfaction on various aspects of job and career, a resilience index (inspired by the pandemic) that measured well-being, social connections and purpose, and a culture index that measured the key elements of our culture that we wanted to focus on—inclusiveness, meritocracy and collaboration. This real-time data in the hands of leaders helps them take actions.

Amazon also has a system called Connections, where employees respond to a question each day, and then every month a report is generated that gives a picture of engagement and mood. Individual managers can also add specific questions for their teams. To focus on inclusion, they have a 'inclusion sentiment tracker' that highlights how inclusive people perceive their leader.[13] Clearly, technology now is a big enabler in understanding employee perceptions and micro-climates.

But these are what employees feel. We can also get actual outcome data on attrition, internal mobility, learning and track those too. Employee perception data, which is real-time, supplemented with actual metrics give us both sides of the coin, and help us think thorough your actions. It is critical that we build this sensing mechanism. My suggestion is not to make it fancy. Keep it simple but ensure it is real-time, measure what is important to you, and track both employee perceptions as well as actual behavioural and outcome metrics.

◆

Suresh Narayanan, chairman and managing director of Nestle India Ltd, on how he engaged his team during the Maggi crisis when, for a few months, Maggi noodles, which made up almost 25 per cent of Nestle's revenue, could not be sold due to regulatory issues:

What were the emotions of people at that time?

The Maggi saga was an existential crisis for the purpose we stood for, a huge threat to livelihoods of our people and a rude shock to the millions of partnerships the company built in its ecosystem, from farmers, distributors, suppliers, retailers, out-of-home clientele, institutional customers and much more! Nestle has been in India for 108 years and we have nurtured a special 'family culture' where career-long employment, pride in what we do, loyalty, respect, decency, hard work and ethics have been celebrated and the company has stood for one strong delivery—unimpeachable food quality and safety in every pack, from every brand, from every machine, each day, month, each shift and each year! This is what we all cherished as a company, and the emotion was one of complete shock, a deep sense of disbelief and a complete unhinging of all that we stood for. People, young and old, were shell-shocked, some angry, others stunned as to how someone could question the very integrity of Nestle India whose foundation was quality and safety of the best kind, which no other food company was capable of consistently delivering. It was like someone questioning the batting capability of the cricketing legend Don Bradman or Sachin Tendulkar!

What were a couple of key actions that you took to get the team charged?

Manage self: My first task was to 'manage myself' and my attitude was, 'It is NOT about YOU and what you achieve or do not achieve, it is about your people whom you cannot let down in the hour of crisis!' This helped me to keep my balance, sense of perspective, minimize the ego and learn to listen.

Manage the context and communicate: I realized that my people (I don't call them employees!) were shattered, some angry, some fearful and many faced the gloomy uncertainty of losing their livelihood. We were at the lowest stage in Maslow's hierarchy of needs, and yet the purpose and spirit appealed to a self-actualizing state. My first task was to communicate, be a shoulder, be an elder brother, a friend, a leader, to assuage the fear, offer hope and constantly listen to how people felt and reacted. I did this through numerous one-on-ones, video chats, town halls, travelling to the marketplace, factories and establishments of Nestle India to meet and converse and leave them with a sense of hope that, 'We shall overcome...

Manage the environment and stakeholders: I have a very simple principle when managing a crisis. Your views are welcome, I will listen, but the accountability is mine as the leader and the buck always stops at my desk! I, therefore, took charge of all external interfaces, of course, with the support of my colleagues. Adversity is the best teacher and I learnt as quickly as I could!

Key learnings from this monumental crisis for leaders:

I have five core learnings from my experience managing different crises over a long career:

1: A leader never leaves his people: Come what may, if you are a leader, your people must see and sense you and therefore learn to lead when and where it matters. This pandemic has defined who the real leaders are and who are just shadows of the visiting cards they carry!

2: Compassion trumps competence: A leader does not have to be the most 'knowledgeable' or the 'most competent' in every field in his domain, but he has to be the most compassionate in a crisis when everyone is hurting, the fog is dense and everyone is fearful.

3: Authenticity beats eloquence: When you lead people in a crisis, it is not charisma or eloquence which works but authenticity and being the person you are with all the warts and moles you carry. No one is a Superman and don't try and fool your people who know that truth!

4: Leadership is asking the right questions, not knowing all the answers: Do not even pretend or attempt to master everything that comes into your domain of information or insight. You are paid to 'ask the right questions' and not 'try and fake knowledge behind every answer'.

5: Adversity is the best teacher; don't waste it when it comes: In my career, I have had to face numerous adversities, big and small, and each time I find myself learning more about business, leadership, about myself, strategic thinking and tactical options while navigating a ship in a storm. You can make the best changes, question the long-held 'beliefs', demolish the 'dinosaurs of legacy thinking' and much more when adversity stares you in the face!

Key Takeaways

- We still take a very 'cognitive' approach to engagement. We need to use the emotions lens too.
- We have a new framework for engagement, a so-called new hierarchy of elements that drive engagement. It starts with having a great team and manager, recognition, learning and career development, psychological safety and finally fulfilling your purpose
- For each of these elements we also have concomitant emotions. For instance, along with recognition, we would see the emotion of pride and gratitude. Similarly, the emotions related to psychological safety are gratitude and happiness. The four emotions of compassion, gratitude, pride and happiness together straddle across all the

'hierarchy of job satisfaction elements'. If these emotions are felt by employees, we would be able to engage them, get the best versions of them at work and get the best from them. Managers play a key role in this.

- Our role as leaders is basically two-fold: inspire and train our managers to engage people by understanding emotions. Establish organizational routines to build the right emotions in the teams and to enable deep engagement. There are specific practices that help build the right emotion and also deliver on the elements of engagement.
- The 'situational emotions lens' is another concept that we can use. For every business situation, we will need certain collective emotions in our people. The collective emotions of a team are a powerful driver for change.
- The insights from the latest research on happiness clarifies that we can build happiness by intentional activities of gratitude, kindness, compassion and mindfulness.
- Engagement in the virtual world needs managers who are more focused on being empathetic and responsive, and who provide clarity and build trust. An additional effort would be needed to ensure remote employees feel socially connected.
- Engaging blue collar workforce needs similar focus but contextually designed practices, given the changing nature of the workforce.
- It is good to have a real-time measure of engagement available with every manager, leveraging technology. A good practice is to get both the employee

perception data as well as relevant analytics from various employee touchpoints.

References

1. S. Surbhi, 'Difference between Maslow and Herzberg's Theories of Motivation', Key Differences, 11 July 2020, https://keydifferences.com/difference-between-maslow-and-herzberg-theories-of-motivation.html. Accessed on 20 October 2021.
2. Daniel H. Pink, *Drive: The Surprising Truth About What Motivates Us*, Penguin Random House, 2009.
3. Tera Allas and Bill Schaninger, 'The Boss Factor: Making the World a Better Place through Workplace Relationships, McKinsey, 22 September 2020, https://www.mckinsey.com/business-functions/people-and-organizational-performance/our-insights/the-boss-factor-making-the-world-a-better-place-through-workplace-relationships. Accessed on 7 September 2021.
4. Timothy R. Clark, *The 4 Stages of Psychological Safety: Defining the Path to Inclusion and Innovation*, Berrett-Koehler Publishers, 2020.
5. David DeSteno, *Emotional Success*, Bluebird, 2018.
6. Sonja Lyubomirsky, *The How of Happiness*, Penguin, 2007.
7. Martin Seligman, *Flourish: A Visionary New Understanding of Happiness and Well-being*, Free Press, 2011.
8. Sonja Lyubomirsky, et al. 'Pursuing Happiness: The Architecture of Sustainable Change', *Review of General Psychology*, Vol. 9, No. 2, June 2005, pp. 111–131, doi:10.1037/1089-2680.9.2.111.
9. Radostina K. Purvanova, et. al, 'Who Emerges into Virtual Team Leadership Roles? The Role of Achievement and

Ascription Antecedents for Leadership Emergence Across the Virtuality Spectrum', *Journal of Business and Psychology*, 24 June 2020, https://link.springer.com/article/10.1007/s10869-020-09698-0. Accessed on 7 September 2021.

10. Barbara Z. Larson, et.al., 'A Guide to Managing Your (Newly) Remote Workers', *Harvard Business Review*, 18 March 2020, https://hbr.org/2020/03/a-guide-to-managing-your-newly-remote-workers. Accessed on 7 September 2021
11. 'The Remote Work Report, 2021', GitLab, https://about.gitlab.com/remote-work-report/. Accessed on 13 September 2021.
12. Sofia Kluch, 'Leading Remotely: What Managers Need to Keep Teams Engaged', Gallup, 20 March 2020, https://www.gallup.com/workplace/296528/leading-remotely-managers-need-keep-teams-engaged.aspx. Accessed on 7 September 2021.
13. 'Employee Engagement', About Amazon, https://sustainability.aboutamazon.com/people/employees/engagement. Accessed on 20 October 2021.

12

We Will Rock You

Building and Engaging a Diverse Workforce

FUTURE WORKFORCE

DIVERSE and MULTIGENERATIONAL

WE NEED TO THINK OF WAYS TO GET THE BEST OF THEM

the key is to build a LEARNING CULTURE that can successfully harness the DIVERSITY

GENDER DIVERSITY

- ✓ Moral need to ensure that we have microcosm of society working

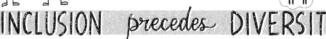

INCLUSION *precedes* DIVERSITY

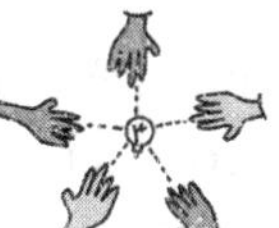

AN INCLUSIVE CULTURE:

- ✓ Grows diversity
- ✓ Leverages power of diversity

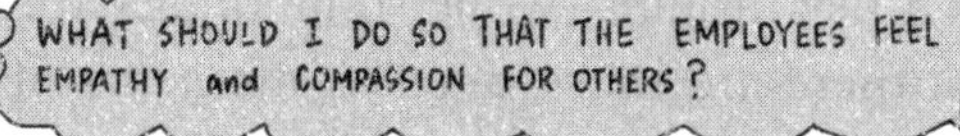

WHAT SHOULD I DO SO THAT THE EMPLOYEES FEEL EMPATHY and COMPASSION FOR OTHERS?

TO ENGAGE YOUNGER WORKFORCE ~

- ✓ Use framework of engagement drivers and relevant emotions

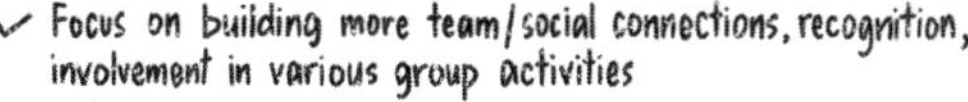

- ✓ Focus on building more team/social connections, recognition, involvement in various group activities

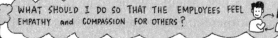

SET THE STAGE BY BUILDING A DIVERSE LEADERSHIP TEAM

A few years ago, a friend who was the CHRO of IndiGo airlines took me to the organization's cabin crew training centre in Gurgaon, where I spent a couple of hours. As you can imagine, most of the people who join as cabin crew are in their early twenties and it would invariably be their first job. They come from far and wide, mainly from middle-class families, with a desire to work and be successful. This was a very diverse group from across the country and, while they held very contemporary, liberal and diverse views, what struck me was their attachment to their families. After the cabin crew training, the tradition is that the graduating batch performs a show of the IndiGo theme song, and the crew are handed their graduation honours by the CEO. Their families are invited to this occasion. This is a great moment of pride for them, and more so for their families. It's a poignant ritual—months of arduous training capped with the touching moment of sharing the joy with their families.

Imagine a workforce with predominantly young women. The way we attract them, engage them and connect with them have all got to be different. But the earlier example brings out a key insight—while some things are unique to a generation, there are those timeless moments of connection and pride that cut across generations, like tapping into the pride of the family in an employee's first job. Therefore, building and engaging a diverse employee base needs careful thought and focus.

I think the case for diversity is probably well made, but each organization has to think why diversity is important to it and to its business. I follow motorsports as an avid fan and it pained me to see the iconic team, Ferrari, struggling during the Formula 1 season in 2020. While there could be many reasons, one major cause was the lack of diversity in the team which comprised, predominantly, Italian male engineers. There are many such cases of failures that stem from lack of diversity, and of successes with diverse teams.

But just having diversity will not help. We need to learn from diverse knowledge and experiences and see how they can be used to improve the organization's performance. Research shows that adopting a learning orientation towards diversity, by acknowledging and using those different experiences to drive business growth and performance makes organizations more effective.[1]

Let's try and unpeel this further. In my view, there could be six broad elements of diversity:

1. Diverse ways of thinking, diverse mindsets, diverse strengths, diverse styles
2. Gender diversity
3. Visible diversity: Race, different nationalities, people with disabilities, neurodiversity
4. Diversity in beliefs/orientation: Religious beliefs, sexual orientation
5. Diversity in socio-economic background
6. Generational diversity: The mix between age groups

In some ways, they are all related and overlapping, but in general a significant contribution to the first element here (diverse ways of thinking) is by the other five: gender, the visible physical diversity, generational diversity, the differences in orientations and in socio-economic background. Therefore, one clear way to build the primary element of diversity in terms of thinking styles is to look for the other elements of diversity. But gender and visible physical diversity is what employees and stakeholders, perceive and experience and, hence, that is important.

However, as we look at gender diversity, there is this natural or moral element that we need to look at. It should be but natural to have a microcosm of the larger population as your employees without any question, so we don't need to have any discussion or business case for women to be equally represented in the workforce. That should be the right thing to do. However, organizations may choose different ways to focus on this, based on their own circumstances.

With this broad context, let's move forward. The first step should be to look at your diversity from the natural or moral point of view and focus on it. Further, to drive greater focus on this, my learning is that each organization has to be clear on 'why we need diversity and what element of diversity we want to focus on', and make that a key thrust. For instance, FMCG companies realized very early on that most of their consumers were women, and that they needed to represent that reality in their own employee base. For many other companies, it is reflective of the population around them and the fact that women constitute half of the available talent. For some others, it is about the values of being inclusive and diverse, something they hold dear. In consumer-oriented businesses, generational diversity becomes important to ensure your employees are of the same age profile as your customers. For global companies, it is about employing people from the nationalities they serve. So, whatever the reason, articulate it. Why do we need diversity and what elements of diversity will we focus on? Communicate it deeply within the organization. A simplistic rationale may not be persuasive—it needs to paint a picture of inclusion, equity, learning and values as a vision of success. However, we also need to go one step further and show in our practices that true effectiveness lies in harnessing that diversity.

Building Diverse Organizations

Over the years, many organizations have managed to attract and build an appropriately diverse workforce. As you can imagine, for each organization, diversity could be a different focus. In India, however, the top focus area for diversity was about getting more women into the organization at all levels, especially in leadership.

Over the last 20 years, huge strides have been made all across India. In 1989, in Hindustan Lever there was just one female HR manager in the company, now HUL has a female HR director and most companies have a majority of women in HR. Take the IT services industry—it has about 38 per cent women, a big jump in two decades. But one area where IT struggles is women in the leadership, where this drops to about 10–15 per cent. At the other end of the spectrum, the FMCG industry has done well in placing a significant number of women in leadership positions. So what could be some of the strategies that one can learn from them? Having met and spoken to many CHROs and leaders, here are my two big moves to grow the number of women in leadership roles: focus on building an inclusive culture and drive career growth for women.

Inclusion before Diversity

Creating an inclusive culture comes before hiring a diverse workforce. There might be some acceptable behaviours that could apply to existing employees but it is better to check if they can cause exclusion unconsciously. Take for instance an all-male sales team. They work hard, and maybe every week they all sit down for a drink—an informal meet where they share experiences and events of the past week. Now, assume you have another male who joins the team, but who doesn't like drinking and skips those sessions. He will feel excluded from the group. Similarly, imagine if a woman joins the team but can't stay back because she needs to get back home. Soon, she will find herself excluded if this late evening drink practice continues. Therefore, you can see that this could be an 'unconscious' exclusion—an existing practice that may not suit newcomers to the team. Similarly, in companies that have a high intensity culture with long-tenured people, it might be intimidating for newcomers as they might struggle to understand the unique language and culture markers and risk feeling excluded. The existing infrastructure of an office also could make one feel excluded, for instance, lack of access for people with disabilities. In the '90s, the lack of toilets for women in the factories and sales depots was a major concern; companies realized it and made changes, signalling a big shift across the organization.

It is a good idea to do an inclusion audit—what are the various practices that are existing and which of those could be seen as not inclusive, and also an audit of physical spaces, company communication channels and people interactions, to identify areas that could be potential 'inclusion' trouble spots. Focus on group discussions with different segments, especially minorities in the company—women, new recruits, people of different age groups—just to hear their perspectives and understand any blind spots the company may have on being inclusive. I have personally found that these are always very insightful.

At the heart of inclusion is a feeling of empathy and compassion. If every employee is sensitive to their colleagues' needs, and goes out to help them, we could create an inclusive culture. This is the key role for all leaders—how do we create the emotions of empathy and compassion in our employees? This can be done by making respect or compassion for others a key behaviour for all employees. Leaders play a big role by setting an example by asking people proactively. Small acts make a big difference. One of the CEOs I worked with would always ask me, `Is there anything else?' as we were ending a call or a meeting, It was a subtle touch to include others in the conversation.

Also, starting any meeting by acknowledging everyone and asking silent members to give their views is a great way to draw people in. Running formal company events like off-sites and conferences by getting diverse groups to have a say helps. Creating various employee resource groups and support groups helps them connect and create an identity for themselves. Regular sensitization workshops on being empathetic go a long way in building an inclusive mindset.

To keep it simple, ask yourself this question: 'What should I do so that the employees feel empathy and compassion for others?' This inclusive culture is the first step to grow the number of women in leadership roles.

If we look at the case studies of companies, such as P&G, Unilever and Pepsi, which that have made strides in moving a significant number of women to leadership roles, we see that they did this by making sure that women are considered for appointment to key leadership roles. Making a couple of bold appointments, even if the candidate is not 100 per cent ready, sends a strong signal. Career growth opportunities are the single biggest block for women wishing to enter leadership roles. So prepare them, give them more development opportunities, more visibility in key initiatives and get leaders to be sponsors of women. The Centre for Creative Leadership's guidebook on 'Mentoring & Sponsoring Women' outlines the difference between mentorship and sponsorship. Mentors give advice whereas sponsors are strong advocates for women's career growth. Sponsors recommend women when necessary and back and support them.[2] We need to have more sponsors for women, not just mentors. We need to break the vicious cycle.

Many women curb their aspirations, either to balance work with other commitments, or by somewhat being discouraged by the perception of the glass ceiling. Making a few bold appointments gives that energy and impetus as more women feel they can make it. Moreover, a solid development programme, with sponsorship will help more women to be considered for these roles. Mandating a slate of at least two to three women candidates for every hire or appointment, gets people to consider women candidates they may have otherwise overlooked. In some industries this may take a little more time due to an overall shortage of talent at those levels, but with clear leadership focus, this one lever will make the difference.

Finally, remove any friction which puts extra shackles on women and inhibits their growth. The post-pandemic world should allow more flexibility and that's something we should utilize to our advantage. However, I am quite sanguine about the future. We have a wonderful base of talent, and I can see women making strong headway into more leadership positions across industries. The one thing that all of us in the society can do is to help them and support them in the traditional expectation of care-giving at home, and free them up from that pressure and guilt.

To summarize, as a leader, ask yourself these three questions:

1. What can I do to enable women to seriously aspire for key leadership positions?
2. What can I do to prepare them for these positions? Am I doing enough?
3. Am I doing enough to sponsor women and appoint them in key roles?

We looked at one example of building more diversity in the organization—that of increasing women in leadership roles. If, for instance, you want to increase your mix of people from different socio-economic backgrounds, the first step will still be to create an inclusive culture. Once that fertile ground is created, you could take specific initiatives to increase the element of diversity you had in mind. Do that in the context of your EVP, that we spoke about earlier. Ensure that your EVP is appropriately crafted for the diversity you want to attract and that your actions are linked to it.

Thus far, we discussed the business need for diversity and how we could build the right diversity needed. Let us now try to look at some tips and insights on how to engage a diverse workforce. The three key levers of engaging a multigenerational workforce are empowerment, empathy and inclusion. Take a company like Amazon India. It has a diverse range of people from across various generational labels employed in its operations team. All their decision-making is document based and substantiated by data. Any person can make a proposal in a document, get views from relevant people and implement it. One of the examples I heard was how one team in a fulfilment centre created an online app to register local villagers for gig work. Whenever there was relevant workload, they would get a message to choose the time slots they wanted to work in, using gig economy in traditional building set-up. An empowered decision-making framework like this enables a sense of ownership amongst the multigenerational workforce.

In the BPO industry, we see a lot of people who join in their early 20s, many of whom come from the interior parts of the country and have been predominantly educated in their mother tongues. In many cases, they would also be the first in their families to work in a company. Their work tends revolve around routine operations, but they need to learn quickly. In this industry, the average tenure of the frontline workers is three to four years. Once we understand the background and mindset of this group, we can try and create personas. I have found that personas help bring in the human element. Think about a person, visualize them and their motives and drivers of behaviour. What emotions do they go through at key moments? What are the key touchpoints in their lives where we intersect with their emotions? Bringing to life such personas helps us think about them holistically and is also a great help in communication.

Let us consider the case of Shanthi, who is joining the workforce. Through sheer determination, she completed her studies and secured a job for herself in a big organization. But this is big new world for her, and even though she is confident, she feels nervous as she joins the team. Her aspiration to secure a better lifestyle for herself and her family motivates her to be a keen learner and do well professionally. She wants to earn more and save some money for her family. Her colleagues are her main social connection and she likes being with them.

When we look at the persona, let's apply the 'engagement framework' and the 'emotions lens' we discussed in the last chapter. They will all apply equally, but what will be different are the kind of initiatives you will need to bring in to meet the same drivers and emotions.

Table 8
Engaging a Young Workforce:
Actions Using Engagement Drivers and Emotions

Drivers of engagement	Core emotions needed	Actions
Great team and manager	Compassion, gratitude, happiness	For this persona, the manager or the team plays a key role in training and supporting. Focus on high intensity, regular engagement of the team lead with the team and ensure that the lead spends time training them. Provide several opportunities for the team to come together, formally and informally.

Drivers of engagement	Core emotions needed	Actions
Recognition	Pride, gratitude	This group is truly motivated by recognition. Increase on-the-spot recognition and visual recognition markers on the basis of various work parameters. Recognize helping behaviours: some kind of peer feedback on who is helping others more every month.
Learning and growth	Pride, gratitude	They need to experience growth in the first few years at regular intervals. A simple learning path that recognizes their learning achievements and rewards them with small gifts. Peer learning and nudges using 'social pressure' like having a learning leader-board for the team. Regular on-the-job catch up sessions with team lead where feedback is given.
Psychological safety	Happiness	The role of the team lead and manager again is very critical: how they solicit ideas and participation and make the team comfortable.

Drivers of engagement	Core emotions needed	Actions
Purpose, achieving goals Personal well-being	Gratitude, pride and happiness	Involve them in team activities or departmental activities where they contribute to the overall company objectives. Social impact activities build team synergies and bring about a sense of purpose. They can be activities like donating books, helping out in a school. Foster their passion and encourage them to achieve personal goals. Expose them to avenues and activities that match their interests like dance, music, sports, etc. Create opportunities to engage with families, even pets of the team.

If we can make them feel, '*This is my place to be*', '*This work is my true calling*', '*My organization cares*', we will be on the road to true engagement. As you can see, just focusing on each group or segment and thinking about them in terms of the engagement drivers and emotions help create the right set of actions. This was just an example, more from some of the insights I had while working with this sector, but equally, this is an approach you could follow anywhere. Remember, at the heart of this, you have to create the right emotions needed. If you or your managers are able to create the relevant emotions, that's it! You created the right engagement.

As a leader or an HR person, as you think about the diversity of the workforce and the multigenerational nature of your employees, there is just one attribute essential for success. That is empathy. Thinking about each group, and understanding their drivers and pressures is critical. That's why the age-old practice of spending a day or so on the shop floor or doing a full beat with the salesperson is so important. We need HR people to take out the time and spend it on the shop floor or office or in the market with people. In fact, mandating a few days a month of such outreach may even help. We are all creatures of habit, and hold many strong beliefs and ideas. We do many things due to the sheer force of habit.

However, as we deal with people who may have a different outlook, mindset or background, we need to consciously hold back our judgement and our natural inclination to respond. That's where empathy helps. If we understand the motivations and drivers of others, we will respond more appropriately. Empathy can be developed; it needs people to have different experiences, meet other people, be mindful and reflect.

One way to do that is to create employee resource groups or affinity groups. Amazon is a good example of affinity groups. Any group of 20-odd people with some shared identity can form an affinity group, get together and make a plan of what they want to get done and help each other with. They have groups like the veterans group (people who have worked in the armed forces), women in operations and families group. During the pandemic, the families groups got together and ran various sessions for their members, from wellness to hobbies. These groups help people connect with their identities.

In the early days of Infosys, the founders were very keen to hear the views of the younger people, and so a Voice of Youth forum was created. These forums continue to have a significant role in the running of each development centre, and come up with great ideas and insights. In addition, Infosys has many clubs and societies that are run by employees—dance, dramatics, running, music, football, cricket and so on. Providing forums for diverse multigenerational workforce to connect with their 'identity groups' and work on common issues help build great engagement.

Diverse Leadership Teams

While we speak about diversity across the organization, one key aspect is to ensure diversity in various leadership teams. The leadership team could be the team running a business unit, division, region or an entity. Ensuring right diversity in this critical microcosm of an organization is important. Why? As leaders, realize that this sends a message to everyone. The leadership team reflects the future of the organization, and the diversity there should reflect the future. More importantly, it helps you take the right decisions, keeping the diverse perspectives in mind. This is not just the 'physical/demographic' diversity, these are true diverse mindsets that we need in every leadership team.

But we don't normally build diverse teams consciously, as it is not considered a priority. But building diverse teams will have a tremendous multiplier effect across the organization. When you are hiring for any leadership team or looking to appoint internal leaders, make diversity a key filter. How can we use this new appointment or hire to bring an element of diverse thinking in the team? Is this team diverse enough? What other elements of diversity can we add to strengthen this team?

Mondelez India is an example of a company that managed to increase gender diversity, especially in their supply chain and commercial areas. **R. Mahalakshmi**, head of HR at Mondeleez SE Asia, told me that one-third of their P&L leaders are women, and one-third of the leadership team in the India business unit are women.

Let's start with the factory in Sri City, in Andhra Pradesh, which was in operation from 2012. It now has 50 per cent women on the shop floor. This was not achieved overnight. They had to go to the villages, where typically the girl child did not go to school after class five, and hire women. They were provided safe accommodation near the factory. These women are now role models and get a hero's welcome when they return to their villages, and this has resulted in villages taking a greater interest in educating the girl child.[3]

In the commercial areas, they started with a design-thinking-led framework, segmented the needs and drove a few key initiatives. First was to ensure that 50 per cent of hires into sales were women. They then created communities internally so that women can lean on each other for support. They co-created gender neutral policies, and established an awareness programme to tackle unconscious bias against women in sales. This was followed by creating special development plans for high potential women to fast track them into key roles. And all this was led by a cross-functional D&I (diversity and inclusion) Council co-chaired by the CEO and the CHRO.

Mahalakshmi notes, 'We can see how increased diversity and inclusivity has helped us make a big impact, both in the organization and in the communities we serve.'

On the same subject, **Sangeeta Pendurkar**, CEO, Pantaloons and Jaypore, remarked:

Whilst there are many dimensions and enablers for diversity, there are two foundational aspects that I feel can help accelerate building a diverse team.

1. **Authenticity of intent:** This is key to building belief and getting people to embrace the diversity agenda. It flows from one's ability to adapt the generic business case for diversity to specific characteristics and features of one's business and consequently, making it one of the drivers of business success. For instance, during my stint in the banking sector, the insight that customers inherently are more comfortable trusting and dealing with those relationship managers who share their own ethnic origin, required banks to staff their frontline managers in a manner that mirrored the ethnicity of the customer base. When this is done well, I have found that authenticity of intent not only builds trust and support for the diversity agenda, it instils a business-specific urgency. It becomes a part of the regular business rhythm. When this is absent, the diversity agenda becomes a 'good to have', a socially correct thing to do or say. As a result, the execution ends up in 'quotas'

for women, in case of gender diversity, which in fact works in a counter-productive manner and can antagonize both genders and kills belief in meritocracy. I believe that building a strong D&I agenda, therefore, requires a strategic 'business-like' approach, with a strong linkage to the organizational strategy with the intent, vision, goals and metrics clearly defined. This should be well-articulated and communicated consistently and repeatedly across the organization.

2. **Inclusive culture is a necessary condition for diversity:** I strongly believe that building an inclusive culture is a pre-requisite for diversity to thrive and flourish in any team or organization. The workplace experience that the 'diverse talent' has determines whether they stay on in the organization and do well.

Think about it—diversity entails different perspectives and thinking styles, resulting more often than not in diverse and disruptive ideas and solutions, thereby instilling a tension in decision-making. When faced with such differences, leaders can suppress them by being directive, seek a compromise solution or work through the differences by being open and inclusive to find a higher order win-win solution. Clearly, the first two choices are detrimental to building diversity, while the third one is a tenet of inclusive leadership and is key to building an inclusive culture.

Hence, very simply put, I believe that inclusion, fundamentally, is about valuing and respecting people and their views without stereotyping or alienating them. This is the most important aspect in creating a sense of belonging in under-represented groups.

Building an inclusive culture starts with the leader herself! As human beings we all carry biases. And to be an inclusive leader, one has to be aware of and very consciously work on addressing one's own unconscious biases. From my experience, there are three key leadership behaviours that can create magic in building a diverse workforce:

1. **Coaching:** It requires leaders to be skilled at knowing when to act like a captain and when to act like a coach. It requires us to create a safe environment where everyone feels liberated and free to speak up, irrespective of seniority or hierarchy. We need to practice active listening and make people involved in a decision feel heard.
2. **Accountability:** Building an open and inclusive culture requires holding leaders in the team to be accountable for D&I, rather than it being an HR agenda. We, as leaders, need to role model and strengthen inclusive leadership capabilities amongst our managers to embed it in the fabric of the organization.
3. **Humility:** Leaders need to have the humility to learn from different points of view and be open to accepting critique. We need to be in control of our emotions and ego, when faced with a counter point of view, even if it is from a junior

employee or a person from an under-represented group.

When I started my career three decades back, being the only woman manager for several years on the team, I was very fortunate to have a set of colleagues and bosses who, through their actions, made it a point to make me feel heard and, therefore, valued. My first boss, an extremely humble leader, never missed an opportunity to ask for my opinion in a meeting, whilst I was still grappling with building confidence in myself. I was treated as an equal and this helped me build a strong, confident, mindset with a belief that the business challenges I am faced with are no different from the ones my male colleagues deal with. This positive and inclusive work environment was foundational in helping me build my career.

Equally, at times, being dismissive about someone's background or perspective can, subconsciously, lead to stereotyping being perpetuated by leaders. Whilst I changed sectors seamlessly, there would be an occasional feeling of alienation and trepidation with comments such as, 'Oh, but she is not from the industry' from certain leaders. This not only destroys the person's belief in oneself, but perhaps defeats the very purpose for which the person from a diverse background was hired! Thankfully, the confidence that I built through several mentors early on allowed me to take these comments in my stride.

The current pandemic has underscored the importance of building diverse teams, since there is ample evidence that diverse and inclusive organizations are more likely to create disruptive innovations and to make bolder and agile decisions—undoubtedly, a critical capability in a crisis and for sustainable profitable growth.

Key Takeaways

- The workforce of the future is going to be very diverse and multigenerational and we need to think of ways to get the best out of them.
- Diversity could be of various forms. The key is to build a learning culture that can successfully harness the diversity we have.
- Gender diversity is important. It is a moral need for organizations to ensure they have a microcosm of the society working. However, to drive action, organizations may choose specific approaches to communicate and enhance diversity.
- In a way, inclusion precedes diversity. An inclusive culture will ensure that we grow our diversity and also leverage the power of this diversity. Ask yourself the question, 'What should I do so that the employees feel empathy and compassion for others?'
- To engage a young workforce, use the framework of the engagement drivers and the relevant emotions. They value a lot of social connections, so focus on building that through relevant actions.
- Building a diverse leadership team, at all levels in the organization, could be a powerful way to set the stage, leverage the power of diversity and get the most from a diverse multigenerational workforce.

References

1. Robin J. Ely and David A. Thomas, 'Getting Serious about Diversity: Enough Already with the Business Case,' *Harvard Business Review*, Issue: November–December 2020, https://hbr.org/2020/11/getting-serious-about-diversity-enough-already-with-the-business-case. Accessed on 7 September 2021.
2. 'Mentoring & Sponsoring Women,' CCL, https://www.ccl.org/insights-research/mentoring-women/. Accessed on 7 September 2021.
3. Shephali Bhatt, 'Inside Mondelez's Best-Performing Indian Factory, Half of the Staff Are Women', *The Economic Times*, 21 October 2018, https://economictimes.indiatimes.com/industry/cons-products/food/mondelezs-best-performing-indian-factory-half-of-its-staff-are-women/articleshow/66297722.cms. Accessed on 20 October 2021.

13

Light My Fire

Realizing Potential Through Purpose

PURPOSE IS 'WHY' WE ARE IN BUSINESS

WHAT BIG DIFFERENCE DOES THE BUSINESS WANT TO MAKE IN THE WORLD?

Why is it important?

PEOPLE WANT TO WORK IN ORGANIZATIONS THAT BRING POSITIVE CHANGE

CORPORATES MUST FOCUS ON 'ALL STAKEHOLDERS', NOT JUST 'SHAREHOLDERS'

PURPOSE must be authentic

BROUGHT ALIVE IN EVERYDAY WORK OF ORGANIZATION

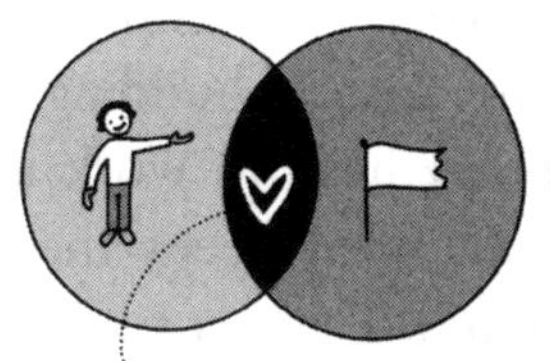

TAP INTO THE INDIVIDUAL'S PURPOSE

ALLOW OPPORTUNITIES FOR PEOPLE TO DISCOVER AND ACHIEVE THEIR PURPOSE

THE SWEET SPOT WHERE ORGANIZATION'S PURPOSE ALIGNS WITH THE INDIVIDUAL'S

ENABLE

COACH

DEVELOP

MANY WAYS TO PROVIDE OPPORTUNITIES FOR PEOPLE TO DISCOVER THE DIFFERENCE THEY WANT TO MAKE

DOING SO CONSCIOUSLY ENABLES YOU TO GET THE BEST OF PEOPLE

Sketchnote: Tanmay Vora

The 26/11 terrorist attack in Mumbai in 2008 ranks amongst the worst in the world. The Taj Hotel in Mumbai was one of the targets of that attack. Some of my friends at Unilever were in the Taj on that fateful night, and I heard great stories of valour and commitment from them. What we know is that none of the employees of the Taj left before any of the guests did. From the manager to the housekeeping staff, they all stayed put, helping guests and supporting the security forces. And when I speak to some of my colleagues working with the Tatas, I hear about the values and purpose that they work for. Trust is synonymous with the Tata brand. The well-being and satisfaction of their guests was important to them and every employee lived up to those values.[1]

Take Larsen and Toubro, one of India's engineering and construction giants, who call themselves 'builders to the nation'. What makes them create such marvels as the Mumbai monorail, other iconic structures and nuclear power plants? When you speak to some employees, you realize the source of their pride—they feel they are part of building a nation. They may not get paid a lot, they have to work in some of the toughest environments, but what keeps them charged is the pride of building the country. There is a larger purpose they are contributing to. We also saw how Diageo became an ethical marketeer of alcohol by propagating responsible drinking, thus creating a groundswell of pride amongst their employees, and this also enabled them to attract diverse talent.

In August 2019, about 180 of the top CEOs in the US came together in a business roundtable and redefined the 'purpose of a corporation', declaring that companies should serve not only their shareholders, but also deliver value to their customers, invest in employees, deal fairly with suppliers and support the communities in which they operate.[2] Of course, a bit late in coming! I somehow find Indian companies to be more broad and inclusive in their outlook towards their stakeholders and communities.

The Mahindra group has a clear purpose that is inspiring and that puts 'doing good' at the heart of its business: 'We are firm believers that "doing good" makes good business sense.' Doing good is a purpose, an attitude and a way of life at Mahindra. A guide for conducting business. These are statements you will find on their website. Mahindra Rise is a great articulation of this purpose, and they bring it to life with their employees, in the community, in sustainability and in getting businesses to focus on doing good.

But what exactly is purpose? Of late, we have been hearing a lot about purpose. We have all heard of vision, mission and values of the company. Vision is about the future goals of the organization. Where does one see the company in the future? Mission is about what the company does and who it serves. In a way 'purpose' is about 'why' the company is in existence. 'Why' are you in business? However, there are no hard and fast rules on how you define your mission or purpose, and we have seen organizations do a mix and match of all of these. What is important is that the organization defines why it exists and what difference it wants to make in an inspirational way.

Let's look at the purpose statement of UNICEF:

> To work with others to overcome the obstacles that poverty, violence, disease and discrimination place in a child's path.

And of Harley-Davidson:

> We fulfil dreams of personal freedom—it's our purpose, and we take it seriously. And while freedom means different things to different people, it's a bond that brings Harley-Davidson customers, employees, dealers, suppliers and enthusiasts together.

It helps having an inspiring purpose. These two examples move you; one with an emotional appeal to the problems faced by children and how you could help , and the other with a vision of freedom. However, your 'purpose' needs to be authentic and believed by the people. And organizations also have to affirm it, and if needed, take some tough decisions to live by their purpose. A recent McKinsey survey of 1,000 managers from the US indicates that 82 per cent of them feel it is important for organizations to have a purpose, 62 per cent of them said their organizations had a 'purpose statement' but only 42 per cent said that their company's purpose had any significant effect.[3] The key, therefore, is to articulate the right purpose and also make it come alive. One of the suggestions is to frame the purpose in the context of the stakeholder challenges in your particular business and also link it to your unique capabilities. H&M is an example. Using its strength of supply chain management, it has led the creation of the Global Fashion Agenda, in which a consortium of apparel companies has come together to work on sustainable fashion.[4]

So why is this important? It helps unite everyone to a common goal. It also attracts the right people to join you, and deselects those who may not be aligned to the purpose. It helps build a common culture in the company. Current research shows that a large number of millennials are inspired by working for companies that have an inspiring purpose and are making a larger social impact.

But there is also a feeling that a lot of this emphasis on 'purpose' is overhyped. Is it really that critical? Are people truly driven by purpose? My view on this is that we can leverage it the way we want. Some companies do a good job and get a lot of mileage from it, using it powerfully to energize and align people, and also as a lodestone for their strategy. However, to get the best impact, I think the key is to additionally engage at an individual level with the individual's purpose. But first let's look at the organization's purpose.

The Organization's Purpose

Some of the best companies engage people deeply—both from the perspective of the company's purpose as well as their individual purpose. We haven't seen much formal discussion on purpose in India, but companies like Tata Steel, the TVS group, Godrej Consumer, to name a few, have been pioneers, and others are now following suit. Here are some ways where the corporate purpose is being evangelized by some organizations:

1. The corporate purpose can drive new ideas, innovation and liberate people to try new things aligned to the purpose. Therefore, it can help be a funnel to determine new priorities.
2. Another way is to align individual or team objectives with the corporate purpose. Ideally, while all work is directed towards achieving the purpose, there could be one corporate initiative that is specifically focused

on strengthening the purpose. That helps connect people more clearly to the purpose. For instance, if your purpose is to work on sustainable ways to meet the everyday needs of people, you may specifically choose to focus on use of water and build some broad goals over it. Reckitt Benckiser (RB) Group's Purpose Council, made up of emerging leaders from 20 countries, is driving change in the business linked to their purpose. RB has set the goal of developing new and scalable solutions to address the challenges of sustainable development.

3. The corporate purpose helps the organization connect with other stakeholders—communities, government, etc., and work out plans that support them. For instance, Unilever's commitment to reduce water usage as well as reduce plastics was a great way to link their purpose to the communities
4. You could have various awards or recognitions linked to the purpose. Awarding teams that have made a difference to the purpose of the organization reinforces the 'why' of the organization and builds a positive mindset

However, engaging employees on discovering their purpose and enabling them in the context of the organization is a very powerful way to drive engagement and the focus on purpose. The belief is that while the company has a purpose, each employee also has an individual purpose, a strong desire to make a difference in some area. Allowing employees the opportunity to discover this purpose and articulate it is very powerful. The sweet spot is when there is synergy between the organization's purpose and the individual's! Here are a few steps that could be helpful in this:

1. Set up 'purpose workshops' where employees come together and discuss their aspirations and identify their purpose. For instance, in Infosys, we created a small team intervention called 'power teams'. One of the focus areas for discussion is the purpose of the team as well as each person's purpose. They discuss for a couple of hours and the team helps each person articulate their purpose.
2. Try and make a difference between passion and purpose. Passion is things that give you great joy when you do them, but purpose is something aligned to your deepest values, the difference you want to make in this world in your own way. Early in one's career, these are all quite fuzzy. I have seen young people talk of learning new things, teaching, community work, working on innovative ideas, etc., as their purpose. There is this *ikigai* definition of purpose as being the confluence of your strengths (what you are good at), interests (what do you like doing) and values (what matters to you), which is also quite useful. What is important is to get them think about this, and a question like 'in the context of your team, family and community, what difference do you wish you could make in the next few years?' helps get clarity. Without getting too pedantic about passion and purpose, try and help people understand what really matters to them most, and what difference they would like to make.
3. Getting to uncover the individual's strengths is usually powerful. Most young people are tentative about their strengths. My experience is that about 80 per cent of the people are not so sure of their

strengths but feedback from their friends and peers helps them realize it. An understanding of what they are good at is important as it gives them confidence to envision what difference they can make.

4. Once the individuals have an idea of their purpose, it will be good to see if the organization can give them reasonable opportunities to work on those. The first step is to see if there are things they can do that align with both their purpose and the organization's. Thinking of their purpose in the context of the organization helps uncover some opportunities. It could be mentoring people, it could be doing community work, it could be working as an expert and supporting other teams; there are a plethora of things that we could work on. Help find those relevant opportunities for people to work on. Well, after all this, there could still be something that is not possible in the organization, and that's fine.
5. One interesting practice that we could adopt here is 'job crafting'. Within available boundaries, it is possible to do a n=1 personalization in terms of crafting a job for your team members, that is, one suitable task for each team member. For instance, if you have a team member keen on mentoring or helping people, try and give them the responsibility of mentoring the younger people or new hires. If someone is keen to make a mark in more technical research, get them to work on thought papers or research projects. In a way, flexibly craft jobs so that it provides relevant opportunities to meet their

purpose or give them opportunities to pursue what matters to them.

6. Provide for various communities in the organization where people could get together to work on areas that matter most to them. From environment to education, from nerdy research to community service, build communities where people can participate. These are normally self-governed employee-led communities.
7. Internal gig work is another practice that is picking up—helping people do things they may be good at, but not having the opportunity to do in their current job. You could create a platform where managers can put up internal projects or peak work demands and get people across the organization to work on these. In a post-pandemic remote working environment, this can be a great way to let people follow and do what matters to them.
8. There are a few companies that let people experiment in areas they are passionate about. We heard of Google allowing employees to work on anything for 20 per cent of their time, and of course 3M has been a pioneer in this with their 15 per cent. This may not be practicable in many places, as there is the risk of efforts going in non-relevant areas, but the principle is something you can experiment with.
9. Finally, following one's passion (what gives you joy) is also important, and there are many who excel in sports, music, dance, drama, quiz and so on. Providing opportunities where possible to pursue these truly works!

My experience is that getting people to think about their strengths and purpose is very empowering and powerful. It truly puts them in the centre of things and gives them huge energy at work. One big insight: the more people think about their own purpose, the more they also think about the organization's purpose and how they can contribute. This truly engages them immensely, if they see alignment of intent!

The millennials and Gen Z who are joining the workforce are increasingly conscious of the impact they want to have and of the social impact organizations are having. Getting this right could be critical for the organizations of the future.

We already saw that the workforce of the future would expect organizations to have a larger purpose and make an impact in the society. Equally, society's expectation from organizations are increasing—impact on environment, inclusion, gender parity, pay inequity, skilling the workforce, supporting social causes, having a voice on the community's problems—and the list goes on. Every organization can play a key role in making our world and our community a better place. Society is an important stakeholder for every organization. The larger the organization, the greater impact they have on society and the more society expects from them.

Having a clear social impact plan is critical, both as a way of giving back to society as well as a powerful way to engage and connect employees. There are various examples of organizations who have done that. The best impact comes from being focused on just one select area and making consistent investment in that over time. Tata Steel, with their focus on all round community/tribal development around Jamshedpur and their mines, is a great example. Mahindra, and its focus on the girl child development through the Nanhi Kalli initiative, is another example of consistent and clear focus. Similarly, Bharti Foundation's focus on primary school education over the years has created a significant impact. The list can go on—there are many sterling examples.

Here is my summary of the key learning from those who have done this successfully. It is critical to identify just one or two contemporary issues in society that would also resonate with the purpose of the company and with the employees. Be consistent in that area; the returns come from long-term engagement. Setting clear ESG goals in that area and communicating your intent are also important. Last, and most important, make that area a focus of employee volunteering initiatives so we get employees to help out. Incidentally, research has shown that employee volunteering helps increase the happiness of employees and creates a greater feeling of satisfaction. A key determinant of our happiness is when we help others.

In conclusion, research shows that for happy and highly engaged employees, they should feel they are following their own 'purpose' and working to a larger purpose, and there are opportunities for them to make a larger social impact through their organizations.

Leena Nair, CHRO, Unilever PLC, shared her experience:

In my early 20s, I found myself sitting in a lab, soldering circuits to insert into picture-in-picture televisions, bored out of my mind. I'd done everything right, I'd studied hard, I'd graduated top of my class with a degree in engineering and now I had a great job working in technology. So why did I feel so unfulfilled and uninspired? The truth is, I lacked a sense of purpose.

In this world of unprecedented change, finding our purpose and helping others find theirs is absolutely vital if both people and the planet are to thrive. Finding a sense of purpose gives you an anchor to be strong when the world around you is full of uncertainty. It fills you with meaning and gives you the confidence to identify the teams you want to work in, focus on what you want to achieve and embrace change as it comes. At Unilever, we believe that companies with purpose last, brands with purpose grow and people with purpose thrive. Our purpose workshops and individual development plans provide every employee the opportunity to unlock their purpose, because we know that purposeful people inspire those around them, take ownership of their work and shape the output of our organization.

The business case for purpose-driven brands is also strong. In 2020, the Zeno group surveyed more than 8,000 consumers across eight markets and determined that consumers are four times more likely to purchase from brands with a strong purpose. Thankfully, companies are waking up to the fact that having a purposeful workforce can determine your competitive advantage, and now 87 per cent of business leaders believe that companies perform best over time if their purpose goes beyond profit.

So, when I look back and think of that bored young woman with her whole life ahead of her, I think of all the other young people out there today still waiting to find their purpose. I was lucky enough to have a college professor guide me towards my purpose when he told me I should be working with people. That is when I changed careers, and I haven't looked back! And now I know my own purpose is to ignite that human spark in those around me to build a better business and a better world.

◆

Exim Bank was in the press recently when they led the work in cleaning the beaches in Mumbai. Former managing director, **David Rasquinha**, on their experience, and how those Saturday mornings brought more benefits than they set out to achieve:

For those of us fortunate enough to be coastal dwellers, the sea and beaches have enthralled us since childhood. The low susurration of the waves in our ears, the salt wind in our face, wading in the warm water and building sand castles, all contributed to opening a new world. Sadly, our children more often than not face not a pristine beach but an ugly smorgasbord of trash; all manner of plastic and other waste obscures the sand and kills marine life. We could try and take back our beaches, or we could shrug and wait for someone else to do it.

Exim Bank invited all staff and family members, from the newest management trainee to the CEO, to be part of this task. Early on Saturday mornings, before the sun became too hot, teams converged on the beach, marked out spots and bent their backs. The aches and pains, bruises and sprains were plenty, but slowly the sand began to appear. Other teams from other organizations and NGOs were working hard as well. Donated equipment removed tons of garbage. At Exim Bank, we posed the challenge very simply. We want a clean beach for our children to play on. Sure, there would be larger benefits to society and the environment, but this condensed goal made it more real for us.

After hours of hard work, the teams would adjourn for refreshments before dispersing. The bonding and teamwork that was seen on the beach was seen in office as well. Apart from the bonding and fellow feeling, there was a genuine sense of equality. I never forced or shamed anyone, but made it a point to be the first on the beach and attack the hardest part. The rest followed. People felt good about doing this. Another benefit was that we also got very good publicity in the media and the favourable notice of our shareholder, the Government of India!

Is the job over? No, as long as people throw trash carelessly, it will not be over. But as long as we can dream of a better future, we will continue to work.

Key Takeaways

- Purpose is the reason we are in business. What bigger difference does the business want to make in the world?
- Why is this important? Increasingly, people want to work for organizations that are bringing some positive change or change for good. There is also the realization that corporates must focus on all stakeholders and not just shareholders.
- Purpose of the organization must be authentic and also brought alive in the everyday work of the organization.
- The biggest benefit is when we also tap into the individual's purpose. Allowing opportunities for people to discover and achieve their purpose is truly powerful. The sweet spot is to get the best alignment between the organization's and the individual's purpose.
- There are many ways we can provide opportunities for people to discover what difference they want to make. Doing this consciously enables you to get the best out of people.

References

1. Rohit Deshpande and Anjali Raina, 'The Ordinary Heroes of the Taj', *Harvard Business Review*, December 2011, https://hbr.org/2011/12/the-ordinary-heroes-of-the-taj. Accessed on 9 September 2021.
2. 'Statement on the Purpose of a Corporation,' Business Roundtable, https://www.businessroundtable.org/purposeanniversary. Accessed on 9 September 2021.

3. Arne Gast, et. al., 'Corporate Purpose: Shifting from Why to How', McKinsey, 22 April 2020, https://www.mckinsey.com/business-functions/people-and-organizational-performance/our-insights/purpose-shifting-from-why-to-how. Accessed on 9 September 2021.
4. 'Our Partners and Network', Global Fashion Agenda, https://www.globalfashionagenda.com/about-us/our-partners-network/. Accessed on 20 October 2021.

Conclusion
The Long and Winding Road

Well, co-travellers, we have been through this journey of looking at how we can maximize the potential of our people through focusing on people outcomes. My idea was not to make the exercise exhaustive, but to spark some new ideas.

But as we all know, this is easier said than done. The question is: how do we make it happen? Is all this practicable? These are, perhaps, the questions going on in your minds. First, what I have outlined in the earlier chapters is clearly very much practicable and, in fact, many companies are already doing it. Yes, there are some areas where we have some newer ideas and thoughts, but on the whole, these have all been previously tested. But why do we still fall short? When I look at this further, I can think of four gaps or areas of losses.

First is the intent gap. Do we have the right intent? This is actually of two types. You may think that it is not worth the effort or given your strategic positioning, you may evaluate that the cost or effort needed are not commensurate with the estimated value you may get. That's fair, as long as it is a well-considered decision. But there is a second type of intent gap where this was not a priority or wasn't seen as important. If you have read this book so far, I hope you realize that the intent is important enough to be a priority, as the benefits of getting the best out of people are immeasurably high.

The second loss is due to the solution gap or the design gap. People are not always rational, and at times the issues are not very clear, and therefore we may end up not designing appropriate solutions. One common mistake we make is to continue to keep changing the process or the system, but are blind to considering changes in the culture or behaviours. So the solutions don't work. The key to this is to go back to basics and ask yourself, 'What is the outcome I am expecting? What is the job I want done?' The second issue is scale; maybe something works in a smaller team, but as you scale it up, you find it floundering. The scale challenge with respect to people is a real challenge. Hopefully, this book will help you with some tips to focus on the outcomes and get the solution design better. But this is a journey—we will continue to learn from our experience to diagnose things better, understand what we really want to achieve and get the right solutions to get the outcome you want. Technology could also help in some way to ensure the design for scale.

The third gap is the execution gap. Anything to do with people also has to be done though people! There are various stakeholders who need to do the right things for you to get the expected outcome. If those people are not able or willing, then you have an issue. The managers play a key role in any people-related process, and where people are involved in decision-making, there will be some subjectivity, which is unavoidable. But the challenge is to think of how we can get managers to be force multipliers, rather than police them. That will call for a very new way of managing people, with more focus on selecting, training and coaching managers, and making them the fulcrum of all people actions. But, most companies keep a balance between managers taking all people decisions themselves and establish some kind of corporate governance to ensure that checks are in place.

Whatever you choose, it is clear that execution of all your people processes and systems is done appropriately through people managers. The leadership of the company is also important: they take the lion's share of responsibility of execution by stating intent, setting an example and holding others accountable. Finally, technology can play a role in execution where scale is concerned. Technology can help reduce the friction to get things done and also help monitor execution.

The fourth and the final gap is the capability or the resource gap. It is both quantity and quality! It may be lack of people or technology to do some of the things needed. It may be lack of budget to carry out actions needed to meet outcomes. The capability of people in the HR function in the organization to drive some of these may be a bit short. What is that capability and how do we build that? Thus far, we have covered some tips and frameworks that one can use, hopefully adding to the arsenal of the team. But capability is more than just awareness or knowledge of what to do. It is about mindset, having the right experiences and also diagnosing and influencing behaviours.

To summarize, here are the four gaps that prevent us from getting the best of our people:

Table 9
The Four Losses

The intent gap	**The design gap**	**The execution gap**	**The capability & resources gap**
Is it a conscious strategic decision not to focus on this?	Do we know what outcome we want and is the design of the solution taking all aspects—the system as well as the people and behaviour aspects?	What are the gaps leading to successful 'embedding' of the actions at scale?	What gaps in resources do we have—people, technology, budget?
Can the business model not afford this focus? Or is it just not a priority? Have there been other pressing issues to deal with?	Is it designed for scale?	How can technology help? What gaps in managerial behaviour and habits should we address to close the gap? What else should the leaders do?	What are the gaps in the capability and mindset of the HR team?

Sometimes it might be tough to quickly identify your gap and there may even be gaps across all four! One more learning from my side: don't bite off more than you can chew. The organization has limited capacity for change. The middle managers, who are crucial to ensure that change is brought about, are already under stress and won't be able to spend too much time embedding new practices. So it pays to prioritize your focus.

To buttress and complement all the tips you may have read so far in the book, there are two critical areas that can help bridge some of our execution gaps—the role of technology and the mindset and capability of the people function.

When I started working, performance appraisal was done in a printed form. You filled it up, made a few ticks, wrote a paragraph and sent it to the HR department. But now you have the ubiquitous enterprise HRM systems which, in a way, determine what your process should be. So most companies are caught between the rigidity of some of these systems and their need to customize. Unfortunately, technology cannot be a panacea for everything. This is where we need to think much more from the basics, using principles of design thinking.

Equally, there are lots of new ideas that effectively use technology. There is this exciting application of 'nudge' technology which will enable you to do the right actions at the right time, thus helping in behaviour change. The role of 'analytics in the flow of work', enabling people to take better decisions based on real-time analytics has increased. Creative use of technology can also help in hyper personalization, making things much more individual specific. Network analysis using various data points, email traffic, etc., can help find influencers and facilitate inclusion of blind spots. There are now a many SaaS-based (Software as a Service) specific applications that could be bolted on top of standard enterprise packages. Depending on your resources and context, you need to think of the best way to leverage technology. Infosys has adopted the Live Enterprise approach—to have many home-grown, cloud-based applications and platforms that sit on top of a standard Enterprise Resource Planning (ERP), but all come together as one application for people to use on their mobiles or laptops.

As the pandemic disrupts how we work, it is safe to assume that many industries may find an increasing number of people working remotely. We will be working more as distributed teams, and a lot more work will be done virtually with an increase in virtual meetings and virtual collaboration platforms. Given this context, the use of technology in our everyday life and with respect to people processes has to move from the legacy HR systems to a set of custom applications that can provide a seamless digital experience to every employee. In fact, HR services will primarily be delivered through technology, a mix of AI powered bots, intelligent self-service, remote counselling services, etc.

I would look at these key principles of technology within the people processes:

1. Be ready for an explosion of technology in the HR area. You need to plan to increase your budget for tech spending.
2. You will need a set of intelligent applications like nudge technology, a very nifty learning application, and employee engagement and wellness applications that can sit on top of your ERP. An HR system is never enough.

3. Even with technology, keep reviewing processes and make them as intuitive as possible. Technology is never the panacea—design thinking is! For the employee, provide one simple app to access all features.
4. Build in analytics as appropriate to enable right decisions in the flow of work based on real-time data.
5. Completely rethink how your HR services are being delivered using remote HR and technology.

Capability of the People Team

Finally, to bring this all together, we need a strong partnership of business leaders and the people function. Unlike other functions, people are at the heart of every business and the most sustainable way to drive people-related outcomes is through a deep partnership with business leaders. With technology increasingly taking care of the operational HR, the role of the HR partner changes.

So what new capability should we in the HR or people function develop for the future? This brings me to the framework I presented in Chapter 3—the new paradigm of HR. Let's do a quick recap.

We have seen that our traditional models of HR need some rethink. Why? The world is changing at a much faster rate than ever, and people—their desires, aspirations and demographics—are also changing. On top of that, we now have a lot of new research which is throwing up some new insights which can power new ways of working and engaging with people. Over these chapters, we have applied some new theories have also looked at some basic ideas and tips. But, to implement all of that, the people function needs to reorient its role and build the capability to play that role. Let us take a look at the triumvirate of roles of the people function and what capability each of us needs to develop to play that role (see diagram on page 39). This is the future focus for the people function. You don't need to be an administrative expert, nor a technology geek. Technology and analytics are very important for you to deliver on these three primary roles, not by themselves.

1. **Inclusive organization designer and advocate:** How do we bring fairness, equity and inclusivity in everything we do? How do we remove any biases, conscious or unconscious? And more importantly, how are we seen to be inclusive and equitable? It's not just fairness in a legal way but in a more proactive, expansive way, giving everyone the opportunity to be their very best. In the earlier chapters, we saw what we need to do to get the best version of our people in the workplace. However, this starts with everyone in the people function. We need to be aware of some of the biases we may be prone to. How can each of us be more inclusive? How do we build our capability to identify biases and remove them? We have to strengthen our capability to build truly inclusive organizations. We have to understand how psychological safety is built in teams and enable people to do that.

   But first, it starts with our mindset. Most of us think we are very inclusive and do not have any biases in our decisions. At least I thought that until I did a 360-degree survey and got the rude feedback that I could be more inclusive! We have to build the capability of turning a sharp lens on our own possible biases and on the unconscious ones in our algorithms, and learn how to remove those through building awareness, technology and analytics. A deeper awareness of where biases can creep in our AI and algorithms and building the ability to correct them would be paramount.

2. **Talent partner and coach:** A talent coach must always be thinking about the right talent, helping articulate the right skills, behaviours, experiences and mindsets (the SBEM mantra we spoke of earlier) needed for key jobs; attracting the right talent, thinking about their learning and development and coaching leaders. The talent partner also helps each employee achieve his or her potential and be at their best. Being a talent partner to the business and coaching people is a key role that the people function has to play. To do this well, each of us has to understand the business context well. Truly understanding the business will enable each of us to design the right solutions, whether it is talent development or career frameworks or learning roadmaps. We also have to keep our ear close to the external world, tracking developments and trends and connecting the dots. This understanding of the business context is essential to get the strategic clarity needed to determine the different outcomes we want and design the right initiatives. Finally, you need to implement them in partnership with the business, which calls for influencing, collaboration and coaching. These are the capabilities needed to be a talent partner and coach.
3. **Emotions/culture architect and catalyst:** We saw earlier that the power of emotions has not been acknowledged appropriately. We have tended to discount emotions and, traditionally, used a very cognitive centred approach to managing change. Emotions are signals to people to

focus on what's important to them, and they have the power to bring energy. The people function has to get a better understanding of emotions and how they could be leveraged. We need to think of ways to create the different emotions of gratitude, pride, compassion, playfulness and happiness that lead to great performance and teamwork. We have to understand how to catalyse change and transformation by leveraging the appropriate collective emotions. These are new capabilities that we need to build in the people function as well as in all leaders. As we saw, collective emotions can be created by relevant organizational routines and practices as well as by leader behaviours. At the heart of this, is the need for high level of emotional intelligence in the people function. We have to set the example by being able to perceive emotions and be aware of emotion management practices.

These three key roles of the people function are going to be critical in the future. HR will have to pivot to these core roles. In fact, these roles would be at the heart of every HR business partner. Building the capability to do these roles as articulated will be imperative for the HR leaders of the future.

◆

Archana Bhaskar, CHRO of Dr Reddy's Laboratories, shares this experience of bringing together a holistic culture transformation:

At Dr Reddy's Laboratories Limited, there were a number of behavioural frameworks and leadership principles that existed within the organization.

There were leadership behaviours, brand promises, principles, yet somehow implicitly employees were bound by the organization's purpose of 'Good Health Can't Wait'.

A cross-functional team of leaders got together to create a simple framework that identified those behaviours which brought this purpose to life at the workplace. What started as a simple task of bringing the different frameworks together ended up being an extensive and iterative activity to come up with the backbone of the organization's culture called 'Aspire'. Aspire (aspirational growth mindset, speed and rigor in execution, people leadership, innovation, results-driven, excellence) outlines the behaviours expected out of every employee in the organization.

Defining Aspire and rolling it out in the organization was just the beginning. It was important to make this the common vocabulary and ensure every employee understands the behaviours in the context of their everyday work and roles. It started with leaders making it part of their conversations consciously. Stories were shared around every tenet of Aspire and through workshops employees across roles worked on defining what each of these meant in the context of their role. To truly reinforce these behaviours, Aspire was integrated in all people processes as well. The performance process was revamped to emphasize the need to assess employees on not only 'what' (goals) they delivered but also on 'how' (demonstration of Aspire behaviours) they delivered it. Today, Aspire is an integral part of the organization and forms the basis on which employees are hired, assessed and recognized. It is also the foundation of the organization's execution system.

In summary, the journey to embedding the culture of 'aspire' in Dr Reddy's consisted of:

- Creating a unified framework that employees can relate to easily
- Creating awareness through leadership role modelling and storytelling
- Enrolling employees by breaking it down to what it means for each role
- Bringing it to life through integration in relevant people and organization processes

◆

Next Steps

This book is meant more as a complete guide for a transformation of the people focus, with ideas to help you maximize your human potential. So, the power of making a comprehensive change in your people function is huge. To do that, get your leadership team together, talk about the ideas and the concepts in the book, think through the lens of the three roles for the people team, identify a common vision, get started on a couple of key priorities and build an HR/manager capability development plan. That will get you started on your transformation journey.

However, I am sure you will be raring to get into action now and test something. Get your feet in the water! Are there some ideas in this book that you would like to work with further? Whether you are a business leader or an HR leader, do think about a couple of areas you want to explore further from what you have read in this book. Also, think about each of the three roles articulated above and the capabilities that you might want to work on. Use this book as a guide, a coach. My recommendation is that you begin with these simple few steps:

1. Think about what are some actions that can be done to create value in your business unit or organization. In which areas can we leverage the people potential?
2. Identify what people related outcomes you would like to focus on.
3. Do a diagnosis and design the solution, keeping in mind the people, the systems/process and the culture/behaviours.
4. Build the capability of the team; assess the capabilities against the three roles and work on a plan to build those.
5. Make a good execution plan; think about the role of leaders, middle-managers, use of technology and communication.

Wishing you success in your journey!

Epilogue

The people function and people processes in any organization are always hot topics of discussion. Everyone will have a point of view on what should be done. Each person talks from their experience, and while that passion can be useful, it can also lead to noise. And, as we saw in that last chapter, your people strategy has to be implemented by the people themselves. So HR is deeply linked to everyday business. Moreover, most people underestimate the impact that people strategy will have in the long term, and may only look for short-term solutions. Putting all this together, you will find that change in the people function is something that needs to be co-created, with enthusiastic organizational buy-in and implemented through people. Hence, this cannot be rushed through. But every little step will count and will make a significant impact in the long run. We have got to be at it continuously and with the right intent.

I hope you find this book useful when you think about how you can lead the transformation in your organization. But it is a journey, and we are all in it together. We all have to keep learning and making improvements, one step at a time. We can amplify that by learning from others and sharing with them. Keep sharing your successes and your challenges on the LinkedIn page for the book!

With best wishes...

Acknowledgements

The ideas and thoughts in this book are a result of my interactions with leaders, mentors, colleagues, teachers and classmates. I owe sincere gratitude to all those people I have worked with and who have influenced me. You have all shaped my thinking, and I am eternally grateful to everyone I have interacted with over these years.

I also dedicate this book to Kalpana and Neerav, my family, who have been in this journey with me over the years.

While numerous people have helped me in putting this book together, I want to specifically call out people who have added their specific insights and experiences to this book. I am truly grateful to D. Shivkumar, R. Rajnarayan, Nitin Paranjpe, Swati Rustagi, Gangapriya Chakraverti, Amitav Mukherji, Manoj Kohli, R. Dinesh, Rohit Thakur, Anuradha Razdan, Girish Menon, Sanjay Kapoor, Alok Nigam, Shreya Bhagwanth, Jackie Koh, Anand Kripalu, T.M. George, R.R. Nair, Ranjay Radhakrishnan, Priyamvada Karthikeyan, Manoj Garg, Smriti Krishna Singh, B.P. Biddappa, N. Krishnakumar, Milind Pant, Suresh Narayanan, Clifford Mohan Pai, Sangeeta Pendurkar, R. Mahalakshmi, Smriti Handa, Leena Nair, David Rasquinha, Archana Bhaskar,

Gautam Sen, Rajiv Krishnan and Anita Miglani. I must thank Tanmay Vora for his wonderful sketch notes. I would like to thank R. Gopalakrishnan, who had suggested the publishers to get in touch with me for a book on HR. I dodged and demurred for a long time, but the pandemic made me think about the book again and I felt this could be my small contribution to the HR profession and to business. Gopal readily agreed to write the foreword, and I am thankful for that. Of course, this book would not have seen the light of day if not for the persistence of Yamini Chowdhury, senior commissioning editor at Rupa Publications, and the Rupa editorial team, which included Anjasi, who helped with this.

A last word: any monies that I receive from the sale of this book will be donated to various charities that aid the education of and create livelihoods for the underprivileged.